THE POETRY TRIALS

FUTURE VOICES

Edited by Sarah Washer

First published in Great Britain in 2016 by:

Young**Writers**

Remus House
Coltsfoot Drive
Peterborough
PE2 9BF
Telephone: 01733 890066
Website: www.youngwriters.co.uk

All Rights Reserved
Book Design by Ashley Janson
© Copyright Contributors 2015
SB ISBN 978-1-78443-998-9
Printed and bound in the UK by BookPrintingUK
Website: www.bookprintinguk.com

FOREWORD

Welcome, Reader!

For Young Writers' latest competition, *The Poetry Trials*, we gave secondary school students nationwide the challenge of writing a poem. They were given the option of choosing a restrictive poetic technique, or to choose any poetic style of their choice. They rose to the challenge magnificently, with young writers up and down the country displaying their poetic flair.

We chose poems for publication based on style, expression, imagination and technical skill. The result is this entertaining collection full of diverse and imaginative poetry, which is also a delightful keepsake to look back on in years to come.

Here at Young Writers our aim is to encourage creativity in the next generation and to inspire a love of the written word, so it's great to get such an amazing response, with some absolutely fantastic poems. It made choosing the winners extremely difficult, so well done to *Aidan Donnan* who has been chosen as the best in this book. Their poem will go into a shortlist from which the top 5 poets will be selected to compete for the ultimate Poetry Trials prize.

I'd like to congratulate all the young poets in *The Poetry Trials – Future Voices* – I hope this inspires them to continue with their creative writing.

Jenni Bannister

Editorial Manager

A POEM IS JUST THE BEGINNING...

CONTENTS

Robyn Anne Stratton (13) 1
Poppy Loosley (12) 2
Julia Whitehead 3
Shannon Keep (16) 4
Shreya Gopisri (12) 5
Shania S Ghosh (14) 6
Jaden-Marie Browne (15) 7
Schinda Blackwood (12) 8
Hayden Phillip Wickland (15) 9
Emma Guest (14) 10
Temitoke Babatunde 11
Libbi Rubens 12
Lilly van Bergen (14) 13
Lydia Smith 14
Safiyah Mahmood (12) 15
Megan McKone 16
Azara Blackwood 17
Joseph Moore 18
Jasmine Rainer 19
Daniel Doherty 20
Ben Marshall 20
Kachaun Nyree Jones 21
Rachael Turner (13) 21
Jack Simpson (14) 22
Niall Paynter 23
Aaliyah Rumana (12) 24
Alice Clare McDavitt (15) 25
Asha Sutton 26
Rebecca Dean (14) 27
Zara Pettet 28
Husnal Mahab Qamar (11) 28
Thomas Broughton 29

Al-Burhan Grammar School, Birmingham
Zahra Safiyya Mahmood (11) 30
Zynah Rafiq (11) 31
Hedika Khalil (11) 32

Aldersley High School, Wolverhampton
Elysia Florence Cork (12) 32
Shamama Chowdhury (13) 33

Beaumont Leys School, Leicester
Nikisha Bhogaita 34
Harley Kirk 35
Henna Gordon 36
Ana Barata 37
Rachel Malemba (11) 38
Poppy Gamble (11) 39
Mollie Winder (12) 40
Ritik Pandit (12) 40
Louis Mobbs (16) 41
Alyesha Chauhan (11) 41
Jack George Baker (14) 42
Ella Harvey (11) 42
Nadine Dorset (11) 43
Jack Fitches (12) 43
Shruti Patel (11) 44
Ella Pallett (11) 44
Avva Shaboull (11) 45
Brodie Potter (11) 45
Alicia Chauhan (11) 46
Weronika Gistinger (11) 46
Tilly Derry (11) 47
Josh Thanki (12) 47
Salimatu Kin (11) 48
Daley Blasdale-Moore 48
Punit Patel (14) 49
Katie Hickenbotham (11) 49
Dhilan Rupen Nakum (11) 50
Caitlin Fletcher (11) 50
Jamie-Leigh Mewis (11) 51
Amar Naliyapara (11) 51
Demirra Green (11) 52
Alex Frith (11) 52
Niam Raval (11) 53
Jacob Canham (11) 53
Georgia Elizabeth Pattison (12) 54
Amber Green (12) 54
Ella Basavci (12) 55
Amy Walton 55
Alfie Cronin (11) 56
Manna Blesson 57

Eden Boys Preston, Preston
Hummaad Badat (11) 57
Hamza Harun Patel (11) 58
Abdur-Rahmaan Adam (11) 59
Faizan Patel (11) 60
Khubaib Patel (11) 61
Ali Ahmad (11) 62
Zayd Ahmed (11) 63
Khalid Bapu (11) 64
Ubaydullah Shahbaz (12) 64
Muhammad Isap (11) 65
Mohammad Patel (10) 65
Taahir Wadee (11) 66
Yousaf Mohammad (11) 66
Muhammad Muzzammil Irfan
Dhanna (11) 67
Mohammed Vohra (11) 67
Aanish Mohammad (12) 68
Sakil Patel (11) 68
Ebrahim Gangat (11) 69
Hanzalah Ukadia (11) 69
Zaid Bagia (12) 70

Endon High School, Stoke-On-Trent
Callum Fradley (13) 71

Groomsport Intensive Support Unit, Bangor
Aidan Darragh Donnan (15) 71

Hodgson Academy, Poulton-Le-Fylde
Isobella Frudd 72

Kettlebrook Short Stay School, Tamworth
Cameron Bishop (14) 72
Bethany Lewis (14) 73

Kings Norton Girls School, Birmingham
Elizabeth Dewes (11) 73
Flora Slorach (17) 74

King's Park Secondary School, Glasgow
Sophie Marshall (14) 75
Susan Jamieson (13) 75

Kirkstone House School, Peterborough
Francesca Clayton (15) 76

Les Beaucamps High School, Guernsey
Ffion Rogers (15) 77

Lightcliffe Academy, Halifax
Katie Hazel 78

Moorbridge PRU, Newcastle Upon Tyne
Sean Robson (15) 79

New College, Swindon
Deanna Dawkins (17) 80
Leandra Inglis (17) 81
Jonatan Akala (16) 82
Liz Malihan (16) 83
Shannon Nicole Harwood (18) 84

Northfield School & Sports College, Billingham
Jamie-Leigh Beaumont (14) 84
Holly Dobbing (13) 85
Lucy Stubbs (14) 86
Lucy Cossavella (13) 87
Niall Watson (13) 88
Annabel Hall (13) 88
Emma Shears (13) 89
Stephanie Otterson (13) 89
Fane Cook (13) 90
Lewis Rogers (13) 90
Zoe Beamson (13) 91
Cloe Laughton (13) 91
William Sherry (13) 92
Max Thornton (13) 92
Alex Jones (13) 93

Olivia Lambert (13)	93
Amy Grey (14)	94
Erin Wood (13)	94
Alex Elizabeth Georgiou (13)	95
Lewis Clark (14)	95
Joanna Brackstone (13)	96
Regan Hoggarth (13)	96
Marlee Taylor (13)	97
Natalie Grace Housam (13)	97

Notre Dame High School, Sheffield

Kieran Vidler (14)	98

Penrice Academy, St Austell

Jake Hemming (12)	98
Megan Paige Stone (12)	99
Jasmine Taylor (12)	99
Savannah Sanchez (12)	100
Tyler Kostov (12)	100
Katie Saunders (12)	101
Aimee Minear (12)	101
Blake Barnes (12)	102
Rebekah Rowe (12)	102
Vicky Fosten (12)	103
Joe Maunder (12)	103
Shannon Burne (12)	104
Joran Rogers (12)	104
Jess Harvey (12)	105

Pittville School, Cheltenham

Penny Cleevely (11)	105
Paris Mary Duffus (12)	106
Luke Smith (12)	107
Jessica Anne Yasmin Burnham (12)	108

Plantsbrook School, Sutton Coldfield

Evie Thursfield (11)	109

Queen Anne High School, Dunfermline

Jennifer Coull (13)	109
Lee Hynd (11)	110
Lily Smith (12)	111
Lisa Van Delft (14)	112
Grant Waddell (11)	113
Ross Inglis (13)	113

Jack Douglas (13)	114
Maisie Pirrie (12)	114
Jody Wright (12)	115
India McKendry (11)	115
Scarlett Dunn (11)	116
Molly Kelman (14)	116
Caitlin Malcolm (12)	117
Brooke Gardner (12)	117
Abbie Susan Gorman (12)	118
Megan White (11)	118
Charlotte Alice, Kathleen Charleston (12)	118
Andrew Savage (12)	119
Kallum S Gallacher (11)	119
Alistair Patten (12)	119
Keela Rutherford (12)	120
Calum Dalton (11)	120
Luke Fleming (11)	120
Tyrone Farlam (12)	121
Calum Law (12)	121
Erin Edwards (12)	121

Rossall School, Fleetwood

Sofia Deplidge	122

Royds Hall Community School, Huddersfield

Jude Blakeley (13)	123

St Joseph's College, Ipswich

Morgan Willetts (14)	124
Madeleine Cooke (11)	125
Helena Chan (11)	126
Matthew Kent (13)	127
Isaac Codjoe (13)	128
Sophie Wykes (14)	129
Louise Humphries	130
Isabelle Atkinson (12)	131
Isabella Grylls (12)	132
Archie Mariani (11)	132
William Marston (12)	133
Harry Smith (11)	133
Grace Ali (11)	134
Taylor Locke (13)	135
Joshua Robert Anthony Palmer (11)	136
William Francisco Scoones (13)	137
Jessica Bryce (13)	137

Rhiannon Dunbar (13) 138
Jack Oakes (14) 138
Oscar Bolton (11) 139
Tom Marshlain (12) 139
Elana Sophia Fraser (15) 140
Alex Mann (13) 140
Reubin Campbell (12) 141
Kirsten Parsons (13) 141
Katie Warne (13) 142
Dominic Terry Raines (12) 142
Harry Suckling 143
Erin Morgan (14) 143
Lily Henshall Howar (12) 144
Katerina Everard (12) 144
Dantay Ward (11) 145
Cameron Towers (11) 145
Leo Bignell (12) 146
Lucy Waring (12) 146
Edward Lucking (12) 147
Patrick Rawlins (12) 147
Eloise Ward (11) 148
Bailey Scannell (11) 148
Chidera Mary-Josephine Nwenyi (13) 149
Katy Heron (12) 149
Nmachi Judith Chidi-Lloyd (10) 150
Reubin Campbell (12) 150

St Joseph's Grammar School, Dungannon

James Fearon (12) 151
Claire McCooey (12) 152
Sorcha Drayne (12) 153
Patrick Murray (13) 154
Niamh O'Toole (12) 155
Rachel McAllister (12) 156
Caitlin McElvogue (12) 157
Oisin McCann (12) 157
Aoibheann Christie (12) 158
Eva Lamb (12) 158

St Luke's Science And Sports College, Exeter

Isabelle Alicia Knight (13) 159

Sanquhar Academy, Sanquhar

Flannery Shay Umstead (12) 160
Heather Frame (13) 160
Keira Marie Cunningham (11) 161

Sarah Fisher (11) 161
Rhiannon Flynn (12) 162
Cameron Carter (13) 162

Stour Valley Community School, Clare

Lilli Simmonds 163
Alban Smith-Adams (12) 164
Annecy Webb 166
Francesca Blackburn 167
Jessica Elizabeth McNaul 168
Morrigan Rimmer 169
Libbie Bush 170
Madeleine Jacobs 170
Lucy Brighton 171

The Aconbury Centre, Hereford

Cameron Tyberious Anderson (13) 172

The Kingsley School For Girls, Leamington Spa

Madelaine Sanderson (13) 173
Helen Lavery (13) 174
Rebecca Blake (13) 175
Gracie Shipley (12) 176
Gemma Hotchkiss (12) 177
Annie Harper Radley (13) 178
Lucie Jones (12) 179
Helena Mannion (14) 179
Shakirah Saquhlan (13) 180
Charlotte Maria Kate Evans (13) 180
Jenna Kate Morgan (13) 181
Lily Constance (13) 181
Harkeiran Sohal (13) 182

The Thetford Academy, Thetford

Annie Lynch (13) 182
Spencer Hornsby (13) 183
Elise Smith (13) 184
Michaela Matasova (13) 185
Annabel Phillips (12) 186
Sofija Zurba (12) 187
Genesis Baker (15) 187
Kieran Dixon (12) 188
Cory Jay Thomas (13) 188
Libby Donno (11) 189
Dylan Thomas Robertshaw (13) 189
Leigh Mortimer (14) 190

Caitlin Gray (11) 190
Dylan Kirk (11) 191
Georgia Shannon Tosney (11).........191
Madison Lorraine Brunec (11) 192
Lydia Dixon (11) 192
Jordan Valentine (11) 193
Kotryna Miliskeviciute (13) 193
Wiktoria Bialek (13) 194
Tomas Diogo (13) 194
Jessica Hendricks (11) 195
Aleksandra Jaworska (12)............195
Abbie-Lee Stevens (12) 196
Kellesha Brown (12) 197
Molly Victoria O'Brien (14) 197
Takitha Marie Malkinson (11)........198
Jack Thompson.......................198
Iris Da Silva (11) 199
Drew Chapman (11) 199
Sharika-Lee Francis (11) 200
Vladislav Bandy (14)................200
David Goncalo Ferreira (12).........201
Layla Lloyd (12) 201
Vera Morgado (11)...................202
Dianne Jayne Wood (13) 202
Claudia Fernandes (14) 203
Shaun Green (11)....................203
Jessica Norkett (12)................204
Joshua Plumley (12) 204
Chloe Crick (14) 205

Thurston Community College, Bury St. Edmunds
Ryan Gooderham (15) 206

Trinity Education Centre, Trowbridge
Emily Robyn Lane....................207

University Technical College Norfolk, Norwich
Lewis Moreton (15) 208

Uppingham Community College, Oakham
Georgia Immins (13).................209

Wolverhampton Grammar School, Wolverhampton
Jasmine Chanian (13)................209
Brandon Taylor (12).................210
Caelan Ferguson (14)................211
Oliver Brookes (11) 212

Wrekin College, Wellington
Henry Phillips (15) 213
Becky Woolley (15)..................214
Isabelle Driscoll (11)..............215
Annie Grimsdale (11) 216
Georgia Thompson (13) 217

THE POEMS

THE POETRY TRIALS - FUTURE VOICES

GREY SKIES?

When, sun nears its end and you look up
And set your eyes on the sky's vast expanse,
Do you see
Black and grey and all the colours of dark?
Or do you see
Pink and gold and all the colours of light?
Because I simply can't think
That people look up at the sky and see
Black and grey and all the colours of dark.
I have to think that, like me, they see the pink
And the gold and all the colours of light.
You see,
In the setting of the sun,
I look up at the low-lying clouds and see,
Not grey, not black,
But purple, and deep seas of blue
Gently folding over each other in a constant wave of dance.
And I see,
On the top of those low-lying clouds,
Not plain light,
But the sun,
Reflecting off them, turning them rose gold,
Like candyfloss on beds of golden feathers.
So I can't think
That you think
That the sky in all its glory,
That has been proclaimed as the ultimate masterpiece of nature,
Is dull
And lifeless,
Because it's not.
Is it?

Robyn Anne Stratton (13)

THE TRUTH OF SINCERITY

Sorry, but yet another word that is in the dictionary,
Time after time it's uttered, sincerity none
And one can lie and lie and live without conscience,
Like day becomes night without weeping away,
About a sin, a sorrow, a sky.

Sorrow, unlike sorry is true, not fake,
It is felt because it has to be, but only by those who are not corrupt,
A population so small, and hated, yet unnoticed and good,
Like the ants, innocent, small, down trodden, never missed,
By you, by me, by teachers, by bankers, by politicians.

Forgiven is a fake wish, we all lie and say we have granted,
We say we have because we want to be loved, not disliked and in debt,
A few say it as it is, but they are not recognised as the words sound the same,
They are sand washed over and ignored by the waves of the pounding sea,
Which is the bully, an enemy, a foreman, a manager, your sister and brother.

Forgiveness comes only in souls of angels and God himself,
Felt because of love, dedication, and often pity,
I try and say that it's OK and believe it, but as a mortal, my heart doesn't let me,
The way bars stop a prisoner from escaping and becoming free,
Because another man has decided that he doesn't like the way he lives.

Perfection is a story told to themselves by the dishonest,
It is just another unachievable goal, that people like to dream of,
But everyone's ideas of perfection are self-centred and greedy,
The way a nib moulds to the style of handwriting, and scratches if another uses it,
It just sets people high, then lets them fall low, so despair can laugh in their faces.

You may despise me for writing this poem, and deem it not true,
So you can revel in untruths that make you happy,
Like every human has done, does, and will do,
Just as the world turns for everyone, and doesn't stop, no matter how sad you feel,
So smirk at me, and hate me, and lie in your head, but you can't hide from the fact it's
Just ... the ... truth.

Poppy Loosley (12)

THE HIPPO

The gentle giant,
Strong and reliant,
The semi-aquatic creature,
Surely has more than one feature.

A hippo's best friend, a big pool of mud,
In he does dive, *splash, splash, thud, thud.*
Crocodile, crocodile his one big threat,
Old hippo recalls the one he once met.

Down he goes diving, deep down out of sight,
The current he must fight with all his might,
His territory he will defend,
Right up until the bitter end.

The secrets he hides,
In those wise old eyes.
Deep, deep he follows his nose,
Deep, deep where nobody knows.

Julia Whitehead

THE SHIP OF DREAMS

Sailing across the sea
leaving life behind we were free
women raising their dresses, careful not to rip a seam
on the Ship of Dreams.

Immeasurable to man
from cabin to cabin the butler ran
it was perfect, it gleamed
on the Ship of Dreams.

It housed all, rich and poor
all designated to their floor
separated by pillars and beams
on the Ship of Dreams.

As we travelled far it grew cold
not suitable for the old
they heated her up, creating lots of steam
on the Ship of Dreams.

Out of the blue it came
no one's to blame
the situation grew extreme
on the Ship of Dreams.

The impact shook the ship
nearly making the boat tip
people gathered in teams
on the Ship of Dreams.

As the water got higher the lifeboats left
people taking all they could, even committing theft
sinking in the stream
on the Ship of Dreams.

Shannon Keep (16)

WHY RESORT TO WAR

This world has a record
For ferocious wars
Just because individuals
Won't abide by the laws
Violence and despair
Both come in a pack
When the situation emphasises
Self-disciplines' lack
The stress people go through
Participants and supporters,
We can only know about
By newspapers and reporters.
There are so many examples
Of what I'm referring to,
Like the Battle of Hastings
And of course World War II
There have been so many conflicts
And unfortunate events
That'll be etched in people's minds
With permanent dents
Like the arrogance of Hitler
Or the Conqueror never wise,
Both men came
With their eyes on the prize
The repeated cause
For the Earth's peace curled,
Is one man's desire
To be king of the world.

Shreya Gopisri (12)

THE LAND OF DREAMS

Close your eyes and imagine a dream,
A land full of chocolates and praline cream.
In a place that is far and forgotten,
Here the soil is marshmallow cotton.

Close your eyes and imagine a dream,
A world of rainbows with your very own colour scheme.
In a land that is unknown,
Here the magical fairy tales are born.

Close your eyes and imagine a dream,
A world full of gadgets and bright laser beams.
In a dimension of technology and funk,
Here you can discover the latest junk!

Close your eyes and imagine a dream,
A domain of magic echoing with wonder-filled screams.
In a cosmos of wizards who can spell,
Here unicorns and hippogriffs happily dwell.

Open your eyes and look around,
A world that you have luckily found.
On the leafy green grass or your soft carpet floor,
This world is yours to explore.

Open your eyes and look around,
The fascinating elements that you surround.
In a universe where anything is possible,
This world is your very own oracle.

Shania S Ghosh (14)

THE POETRY TRIALS - FUTURE VOICES

ARMOUR OF WORDS

My mother told me she loved the colour of the sky.
That day the sky was a canvas of colour
painted just to make her smile.
The next day she told me the sea was a calming place
But when I sailed to the sea to calm my nerves
Each wave felt like a personal assault
carried out just to prove her wrong.
My mother told me if I stayed low on the ground when lightning struck
I would be safe but the day the sky turned grey
And lightning came striking down
It hit me even though she promised I would be safe.
The day after I was hit, the sky was a smudge of ugly
With clouds and bullets shooting from them
Whose target was the patch of grass I called my haven.
When cold came around and the snow started falling
My mother was there to tell me if I wore the clay coloured coat she got me
I would be shielded from the winter that wished to harm me.
My mother's words were always welcome in times of struggle.
My mother's words were laced with love and stitched together with only good intentions;
But my mother's words were only links in the chainmail
I had built around myself to protect to me,
to be truly strong,
I still had to walk into battle and survive.

Jaden-Marie Browne (15)

LET THE GAMES BEGIN

They were all tall, taller than me,
axes, knives, daggers you see.
The odd anxious one is always left out,
as obnoxious sleep knocked some out.
It hadn't started, that's all I knew,
all the lads picking on others leaving me and a few.
The anger and terror grew up in a fight,
but all I wanted was the light.
I wanted to cherish my moments all alone,
but the big boys said, 'You're never going home.'
I wanted to crack out of my undefeatable shell,
but if I did this it would be hell.
I wasn't gonna survive a single bit,
as love fell and hatred lit.
Life wasn't fair, I always knew that,
everyone treated me like a doormat.
The warnings came like a telegram,
I felt like a newborn lamb.
I have no one left in my life,
as I glared at myself on my knife.
I saw the chief's head rise up,
Like I was the water trapped in a cup.
I knew what was gonna happen as I cowered away,
looking in his eyes I knew what he was about to say.
His chest rose up as the lights grew dim
and bellowed let the games begin.

Schinda Blackwood (12)

FUTURE EARTH

The near distant future Earth
Every tree has been destroyed
All of nature is gone
The seas turned into deserts
Oxygen has become extremely rare
Why didn't we listen earlier?

We built lots of factories
Made lots of horrible gases
Just because we became nasty
And greedy businessmen took over
Who destroyed our beloved planet
And ignored the public's opinion.

There were people who tried
To help humanity get cleaner
But they ended up failing
And most humans all perished
We thought we were invincible
But sadly nothing lasts forever.

The last of the human race
Moved to a new planet
To start a new civilisation
One that lives in harmony
One that respects nature
Also known as New Earth.

Hayden Phillip Wickland (15)

50/50

I like this place because it's a second home, a place to have fun
With friends that seem more like family.
It's an escape from my own home.
It's where I won't be judged.

I like this place because it's a second home.
The people are helpful and kind,
The many ornaments shine at me,
Grinning, smiling, waving.

Listen to the sound of my laughter
And others too.
The clangs of pots downstairs
And the hum of music mixing with the television.
The birds sing, barely heard
And cars join the tune, an unequal beat.

I like this place. I can forget the worries of being judged.
I like this place. I can remember the moments that mean the most.
I like the place. I can feel comfortable in my own skin.

I like this place, because it's a second home,
Where I have slept on the floor more than once,
Where I have baked cakes and ate more,
Where I have forgotten about my sadness,
Where I have been happy, where I shall be,
Once again.

Emma Guest (14)

THE LIAR'S CHARM

Darkness is written all over him
But I will stay
Blood is coated all over him
But I still remain
As I have been caught by the liar's charm

As you stand with your devious smile
I can't help but say
You're the reason I couldn't walk down that aisle
And never regretted that day

You were always gone, removed from my sight
But when home you were a monster in my bed
That's why I left that night
Leaving you dead

I stabbed you several times
I spat on you until you wept
That night I committed my crimes
It was something I had to accept

Maybe I shouldn't have picked up that knife
But I couldn't handle your lies
And never could be your wife
I still feel pity on your cries
As I am the liar's charm.

Temitoke Babatunde

FINAL THOUGHTS FROM AUSCHWITZ

People may be different
No one is the same
But there is no such thing as peace
Someone has to take the blame
Lying there, useless
Floundering in the waves
But the ocean is big
God picks who he saves
We are a shield
We fight, we fall
But nothing is indestructible
We will always stand tall
Your throat is closing up
Your tongue is getting dry
The world is closing in
There's no energy to cry
Veins are running slowly
Like broken pipes
And the last thing you see is
Stripes, blue and white stripes.

Libbi Rubens

THE POETRY TRIALS - FUTURE VOICES

ANGER IS A SHORT MAN

Anger is a short man, with a red suit and tie
Piggy eyes, a short-tempered guy

Confusion is an old man who makes every light go dim
Bewildered, staring at everything around him

Happiness is a small girl with big eyes
They are as blue as the sky where she flies

Jealousy is an old woman haggard and hunched
Wearing a guilty dress that is creased and bunched

Excitement is a young boy with white hair and clothes
Never stops running, never slows

Sadness is a girl in a frayed black dress
Sat in the corner, trapped in a whirlwind of distress

Fear has a black robe and milk coloured skin
It stays silent slowly drifting, fingers sharp as pins

No matter, where you are, how you are, one is in control
Throughout your life as a whole

And no matter what you do they are always there
But emotions are nothing to scare.

Lilly van Bergen (14)

MONSTERS ARE HUMANS

His eyes pierced through my skin
and washed away the trail of hope,
buried in my veins.

His battered arms, proved
his reputation, was anything
but a myth.

Each wound, had parts of his
soul spilled into it.
Revealing the shattered remains
of himself left behind.

The claws, which were his hands,
intrigued my mind, and screamed
a story, I craved to hear.

I awakened from my dream,
with no clue what reality is any more
and realised, that the only monsters in this world,
are also humans too.
We spend so long, hiding away from a fantasy world,
when the real danger in our lives is ourselves.

Lydia Smith

FOX

Fox,
Moonshine,
Creeping across ferns of crimson ash.
Wild winds hurl forward across bushes
Causing a sea of dribbling rain, gushing flow.
Pauses, pauses and sniffs the air which hangs above
Red heads or fluffy fox fur.

Fox,
Moonshine,
Whirling winds.
Padding paws as furry as a snowy blankie.
Food, food smells fill a whiff of air,
Crashes of bricks falling. Racing in and back.
Foxy fur creeps under a bush. A chicken hangs from his drawn back lips.
Beginnings of a snarl and a hiss.
Racing away.
Moonshine,
Fox,
Goodbye.

Safiyah Mahmood (12)

I REMEMBER

I remember the bruising on my skin,
touching it felt like clutching a pin.

I can still remember being locked out in the snow
while you taught him how to throw.

I can even remember being locked in a cupboard, squeezed by the dark,
afraid and waiting to hear your bark.

I remember the isolation,
the feeling of desperation.

I remember the first time you drew my blood,
I spent a week hidden by my hood.

And even after it all
I used to run back at your beckoning call.

But now I won't because you're the one alone,
I hope it hits you like a mound of stone.

You've lost your only daughter now,
I hope you're happy, I hope you're proud.

Megan McKone

FRANKENSTEIN

You can't create a monster and then condemn it,
Curse it, judge it, hate it.

You made it.

Each part carefully constructed
Joined together by bolts of bitterness,
Each malignant feature delicately mapped out
This is your design, you made it
It can't be pushed to the side and left there.

It must be nurtured
It must be fed
Or else it'll be misled.

You can't create a monster and then condemn it,
Curse it, judge it, hate it,
That will change it.

Lost, it may turn, consumed into the entrancing caliginous side.
You can't create a monster and then condemn it,
Curse it, judge it, hate it.

Azara Blackwood

3DM GEAR

You soar through endless skies,
yet you have no wings,
your heart racing
and your mind ablaze.
Sweat, blood, tears,
the very least of your worries now.
Choose to dwindle and you'll be eaten,
turn to fight and be slain.
Fly, grapple, swing, cry, die.
Time to find out . . .

Dare to live through death
for the sweet victory of nothing.
Knuckles white
blood red,
death could never have been so blissful.
Yet you cling to life with such fondness
for no one and nothing.
Pray, hope, soar, hide, live!

Joseph Moore

THE MOUNTAIN

Free like a bird,
You soar high above humanity.
You venture into unknown territory.
Completely at one with nature.

Sitting above the clouds,
Looking down on scattered rocks,
Green grass shoots up amongst the grey.
Completely at one with nature.

Look down.
Your heart races as you edge up the rock face,
The wind howls past.
Busy roads become distant as you climb closer to Heaven.
Completely at one with nature.

Forget your problems.
Your worries.
Escape the vicious grip of society.
Completely at one with nature.

Jasmine Rainer

THE GLASGAE HORROR

Tons o people doon in George Square
Six o them ended up hittin' the flair
The driver's heed on the wheel
The people listen to them squeal
People running away like flocks o birds
They were so big I'd call'em herds
Happy people heads held high
Turned to frightened people och aye
The police are 'ere, driver awake
He's so still he cannae even shake
The lorry still goin' naebody around
Bang! Crash! What a loud sound
People watchin' the news, nae fitba the night
And when they watched it was a bad bad sight
Three members of a family o where's ma cell?
The mother comes oot the shop when she gets the tell
It's New Year's time, one month past
Let's see if anything happens and if it's worse than the last.

Daniel Doherty

TIME

Relaxing on the warm barren beach
Watching the sea shimmer in the sunlight.
Time ticking away,
Seeing the fluffy clouds float by.

Listen to the sound of my beating heart
Waves crashing on jagged rocks.
Hear the sound of children laughing,
Letting the time tick by.

Forget the troubles of school and work,
Remember your childhood
And all of the fun times.
Letting the time tick by.

Ben Marshall

DARKNESS IS ALL

As we cry for the light
And swell up at night
We think about the slaves that try to fight
Life is a disaster that is retrieved by people we don't like
We are worn out and passed down so that the master's money can be turned around
As we climb for the light that will never be in sight
As we dig for the freedom which will never become right
We try to run
And try to build
A trust that cannot be sealed
The love for us is just whips and carriages
As we just feel like a heavy load of baggage
As we cry for light
And swell up at night
We think about the slaves that try to fight

Do you see what life is like?

Kachaun Nyree Jones

CANDLELIGHT

Darkness all around me,
All alone in the quiet, still night.
Not a word I can hear as I tiptoe to the kitchen.
The squeaking of the drawer breaks the silence:
Click, click, there . . .
A little flicker of light appears; I feel safer now,
Now there is light.
And, suddenly, the little flame is gradually getting bigger and bigger,
Until I can see all around me.
I get the feeling of warmth rushing through my blood;
I am not alone and in darkness any more.

Rachael Turner (13)

HURT

Every morning I get out of bed
To face another day of dread
I walk to school
Where people start to be cruel
In lessons they are very verbal
Thinking they are in the winner's circle
Finally it's lunch
But I hide away so I don't get punched
They say stuff about my mum
And make me feel like scum
My name's Bill
But they're the ones I want to kill
Pulling on my shirt
Which really hurts
They make me pained
Which makes me feel drained
When will they stop?
I just want to know before I drop.

Jack Simpson (14)

IF YOU AIN'T ME, DON'T HATE ME

Our world judges people by
The way they talk or walk
Their mouth is a weapon
And say what they want with no apologies.

But why do we live like that?
In a world where everyone's different
How can you choose who they are
Because we can't understand them?

So we shout and discriminate those
Of us that make the change
They have their life why don't you
Don't be scared of anything.

I guess it's all in our bloodline
This ain't no one line
One hand on the Bible, I ain't in denial
Live your life, any way you want.

Niall Paynter

THE 31ST OF OCTOBER

'Tis the end of October
Withering trees drop down pinecones:
To welcome the eve of November,
The bees let out deepening drones.

Joyous crowds huddle in tribute,
To the end of the month's successful yield.
Now the growers sell their ripened fruit,
Whilst lively children run merrily on the field.

Groups join together in their spooky costumes,
For the receiving of their sweet loot.
Girls giggle on their wooden witch brooms,
Trying to be frightening, but they still look cute!

Now dusk is leisurely descending,
The tired now stroll drowsily.
This Halloween is forlornly ending,
Whilst minds die sleepily . . .

Aaliyah Rumana (12)

THE POETRY TRIALS - FUTURE VOICES

THE LIGHT IN THE DARKNESS

The light dimmed.
It was dark on the streets.
Spiders scurrying in murky corners.
Wispy webs flapping in dusty silence, clinging to the wall with ghostly fingers.
No light to guide my way.
I was starving. Shivering.
Dying.

I didn't want to walk into the light.
People walked past. I wasn't 'human' – to them.
I was an invisible ghost.
Then the light shone down.

He reached out his hand. Then there was food and warmth.
I wasn't starving. Shivering. Dying.
I saw the light in his brown eyes.
It was the light of Christ.

Alice Clare McDavitt (15)

JUST LET GO

So he looked to the sky
And smiled at the sun
Because being positive is something that should always be done
He let go of all the hassle
And the things that he didn't need
Because life is too short, too short indeed
So when you have problems
That are just eating you alive
Remember you only live once
It's not a dress rehearsal, it's live
We should live a little
And thrive
To be better in ourselves
Because life is a pretty beautiful place
And so are you for that matter
Every part from your feet to your face.

Asha Sutton

THAT GIRL

The one girl in the back row,
Filled with sadness and sorrow.
But upon her face lay the beautiful smile,
Even though it showed different in her file.
Months and months of beatings,
But she kept going.
She lived,
Even though she should have been loved.
The one she trusted was a lie,
That's when she started to cry.
She slowly became quiet,
And went on a diet.
Finally she broke,
As she tied the rope.
She said goodbye,
As she thought of the reasons to die.

Rebecca Dean (14)

DO YOU KNOW ME?

Do you know me? The real me.
I'm sick of people acting like they know me, because no one really knows anyone.
What really annoys me is that people have the nerve to judge you,
But they don't know you, they don't.
People don't think that waking up every morning is a struggle,
Not just physically but mentally.
People don't know, people don't care, it's just not fair.
People assume that everything is perfect
And that I'm fine but they don't know anything.
When I get into trouble, they instantly think it's a crime.
Now I'm running out of time, it's getting too much,
I'm finding it hard to stay focused when so much is going on.
People just think everything's normal, everything's fine, but is it?
Do you know me? The real me.

Zara Pettet

SISTER'S LOVE

Side by side, or miles apart,
Sisters will always be connected by the heart.
A sister brings sunshine to brighten your day,
A sister brings joy through her loving ways,
A sister is a blessing that comes from above,
A special and beautiful treasure to love.
Sister to sister, we will always be,
A couple of nutshells, from the family tree.

Husnal Mahab Qamar (11)

UNTITLED

If you are smart, you would be with us.
You might think that we are a myth
But I'll tell you, we aren't.
For we are Castitas, and we are the best.

We study all and benefit from them.
Even the smallest of things will reduce the bill.
For we are the Castitas, and we are the smartest.

Learning about the leaves where light ponders through.
We benefit from this, and we get a one-way road.
For we are Castitas, and we're super smart.

If we had to fight
Our technology would be right
And our jobs will fall.
For we are Castitas, and we are the strongest.

Thomas Broughton

THE AXE

On a dark and ghastly night,
When the moon was at its peak,
I turned around the corner,
And met an ugly freak.

His face was thin and pale,
And his hair was as black as coal,
And on his gruesome face,
Was a very ugly mole.

And then I saw in his hand,
Was a big, glinting axe!
Dripping with his ear wax,
The colour of unhealthy Pepsi Max.

I closed my eyes and waited,
For my spirit to rise . . .
Slash!
And then I met my demise.

But no I looked up in surprise,
And what I heard brought tears to my eyes,
He spoke kind words,
That made my cheeks flame,
And brought me a lot of shame,
How things for him would never be the same.

He once had a daughter called Jane,
She was the apple of his eye,
But oh my, oh my,
How she changed her ways,
By spending all her days,
In such a dreamy haze.

The company she kept,
Was one you would have left,
As they dealt with drugs,
Which scarred their ugly mugs.

Soon after she died,
She never became a bride,

Her dad cried and cried,
And that was the end of his cheerful side . . .

So just you make sure,
You don't open the wrong door,
And stay away from breaking the law,
Because you might hurt your family like a chainsaw.

Zahra Safiyya Mahmood (11)
Al-Burhan Grammar School, Birmingham

PLEASE!

I can't take no more
I can't stand it!

All the days you say
You don't mean it!

But I know you do
Oh yes you do!

Why do you always annoy me
Can't you leave me alone for one day please!

I need a break
And a chance!

I get low grades 'cause of you!
I don't need this stress any more please!

Leave me alone and let me study oh yeah
Why don't you get out of my life!

And let me go on my ambitions
I wanna win please!

Zynah Rafiq (11)
Al-Burhan Grammar School, Birmingham

THE ROBBER OF THE NIGHT!

There is a robber on the street
Which you should never meet
He rapidly comes at night
When there is no light.
He has jet-black hair
Don't go near him or he will bite you, just like a bear.
He can be very scary
His favourite fruit is the pear
He eats it just like he doesn't care

Hedika Khalil (11)
Al-Burhan Grammar School, Birmingham

KITTY CAT

Kitty cat, sneaky and sly
Kitty cat, watch him with your eye
Kitty cat, you're very, very clever
You have nine lives, you'll live forever.

Kitty cat, kitty cat, be cautious of this beast
Kitty cat, may hunt you down for a midnight feast!
Kitty cat, kitty cat sneaky and sly
You have nine lives, you'll never die.

Kitty cat, oh kitty cat, your time has indeed come
What little you spent with us, was quickly done
Kitty cat, my kitty cat, you'll live forever!
In our hearts, where you'll never sever

Elysia Florence Cork (12)
Aldersley High School, Wolverhampton

DO YOU KNOW MY FRIEND DEPRESSION?

Do you know my friend, Depression?
He is with me all the time.
He is the reason I feel weak
And the reason why I want to cry.

When I'm all alone
He tells me I have no friends.
But when I'm in front of people
He tells me, 'Go on, just pretend!'

I can't tell people what happens
It's all between him and me
I feel foolish as I believe him
And blind for what I can't see.

I have people who care
But he tells me they don't.
'They only treat you as a charity
You have no hope.'

Have you seen my friend Depression?
I haven't seen him around.
I don't hear his voice in my head
It's bringing me down!

I don't feel like crying
I don't feel sad
I can control my feelings
I am breathing at last.

If you see my friend Depression
Tell him I found a new friend.
She is called Happiness
And she doesn't tell me to pretend.

Shamama Chowdhury (13)
Aldersley High School, Wolverhampton

LIVING WITH REGRET

One day my mum said,
'Please spend some time with me, dear,'
But I was busy.

Then she kindly asked,
'Please can you make me some tea?'
But I was busy.

My mum understood,
She went into the kitchen
And made her own tea.

My mum then asked me,
'Do you want to watch a film?'
'No Mum, I'm too tired.'

My mum understood,
She watched the movie alone
And then came upstairs.

She asked me softly,
'Shall I read you a story?'
'No Mum, I'm too old.'

That night, I felt bad,
I should have spent time with Mum,
'I will, tomorrow.'

I woke up early
And ran into my mum's room,
But she was asleep.

Her face was quite pale,
She lay gracefully, eyes closed,
Her body lifeless.

'Mum,' I cried, 'I'm here,'
'I love you, Mum. Please wake up.'
But it was too late.

Nikisha Bhogaita
Beaumont Leys School, Leicester

ELDER'S PENCIL CASE

In your hand is your pencil case,
Filled with many tools and decisions,
Only you, Harley, can decide them
And tie the final lace.

In there is a ruler,
There's no need to measure yourself up against society,
Everyone is perfect in their own way,
You don't need to be any 'cooler'

In there is a rubber,
Erase away the people that weigh your life down
And never look back,
You're not the window scrubber.

In there is some empty pens,
You will lose important people in your life,
But Harley, remain strong,
If you need help, always turn to your friends.

In there are some paper clips,
Link with other people
And unite as a team
And you can be the one riding the success ship.

In there is some sticky tape,
Stick by the people you love and respect,
As they are very important to you
And make sure they never escape.

So dear future self,
Take your pencil case with you
And learn from your mistakes
And never forget it on the shelf.

Harley Kirk
Beaumont Leys School, Leicester

DARLING

Here darling, take a tissue.
Wipe off that make-up you're hiding behind
The hate, the ferocious pain, you always tried your hardest to conceal
Being the foundation in the fake girl's lives, even when it was nothing you could heal.
Powdering over the potential that always shone through
Why cover the real self? Why cover the real you?

The mascara you always applied is another issue
Take a make-up wipe this time, it will help.
Those spiteful girls' comments, they could always make you cry
But you would hold it together, so the black marks wouldn't run dry.

Seriously though, I'm glad the lipstick stopped
Take a wet cloth; it should soon take that off.
The nude lip liners, peachy lipsticks, made you smile beautifully, but God wasn't that fake
Tell me darling, was that for the mean girls, or was it for your own sake?

So please darling, take off that make-up
Wash that face. Scrub it until you are clean
Even though you applied the make-up thickly, I saw yourself cracking through
The girls tried to shape you, they almost changed you, I knew it wasn't true
But now you are without it, you are finally free; you're yourself and you can finally be you.

Henna Gordon
Beaumont Leys School, Leicester

THE POETRY TRIALS - FUTURE VOICES

ENJOY LIFE WHILST YOU CAN

Dear past me,
enjoy life while you can.

From me to me,
how times have changed.
Like a boat on the sea,
isn't it strange?

You go from one friend to another,
learning from your mistakes,
but it is always your mother
who fixes what you break.

I am sorry to say
that time does fly by,
tomorrow isn't today,
so open your eyes.

One thing you need to understand
is that people will mistreat you,
but your body is a temple placed on land,
so do not let that drive you askew.

Aim high and love yourself,
because only you can achieve wealth,
not with riches brought upon oneself,
but in valuable company and good health.

Dear past me,
enjoy life while you can.

Ana Barata
Beaumont Leys School, Leicester

DEAR FUTURE SELF

Be kind to others
Don't judge yourself by someone
With age comes wisdom.

Then to have never lived
It is better to have lived
Live it while you can.

Respect your elders
You don't know when they are gone
Love them forever.

Love your family
Don't be shy, spread the word kindly
There are people out there.

You have a long way
Your journey is not complete
Don't worry, okay.

You are really good
Cherish the memories okay
The past is the past.

Now is the present
So remember all the things
Achieve to be the best.

Rachel Malemba (11)
Beaumont Leys School, Leicester

DEAR FUTURE SELF

I have some advice,
That I can absorb deeply,
In twenty years time.

Haters are jealous,
Good giving grateful getting,
Forgive don't forget.

Be friends with many,
So you'll have no enemies:
No need to worry.

Concentrate always,
Do your best to improve skills:
Nobody's perfect.

Accept who you are,
Don't wear make-up: you'll feel fake . . .
Accept your beauty.

Don't regret a thing,
Life happens for a reason.
Be you, be unique.

Is life going good
Future me? Do I have kids?
Live life whilst you can . . .

Poppy Gamble (11)
Beaumont Leys School, Leicester

FIREFLY

It's almost May
And yesterday
I saw a firefly.

You don't see
Them a lot
In the city.

Sometimes in
The park
In the near dark.

One comes out,
You'll hear a little kid shout,
'Lightning bulb! Firefly!'

It's almost May
And yesterday I caught
A firefly in my hand.

First firefly I've seen
In a long, long time.

'Make a wish,' Miss Edna said,
'Make a good one.'

Firefly wishes always come true.

Mollie Winder (12)
Beaumont Leys School, Leicester

SPACE!

The big bang, the loudest explosion,
Space, the darkest thing in the world.
The stars are the only brightness in the sky,
They shine bright like a diamond, nothing more, nothing less.
Planets circling around stars,
Spoosh, spoosh, rockets flying in the air,
Zero gravity keeps you in the air.

Ritik Pandit (12)
Beaumont Leys School, Leicester

FUTURE EXPECTATIONS POEM

Everyone dreams of a future with wealth,
But nobody knows how to prepare themselves
For what the future will hold and how it will turn out,
Money isn't really what it is all about.

People all want fast cars,
People all want gold bars,
People don't think realistic,
People get reality and twist it.

In reality none of this seems to occur,
It's just a dream, just a blur,
People living their life anxiously,
Waiting for their dream fantasy.

The future is not like people think,
It is like a blur, you'll miss it if you blink,
When the future comes it will be a shock,
There's no way to hide, there's no way to block.

In reality it's harder than you believe,
But to get it good, you have to achieve,
Then you work your way up
And use the people around you to make sure you don't get stuck.

Louis Mobbs (16)
Beaumont Leys School, Leicester

BEACH

The sandy beach and the breeze is swaying by,
Little children playing in the smooth sand,
The howling wind passing,
There are lots of children nattering and laughing
And in sight the sea is rolling over,
Ice cream and tasty hot doughnuts in the distance,
The refreshing smell of fish and chips on the pier,
Also the magical water flowing.

Alyesha Chauhan (11)
Beaumont Leys School, Leicester

LUPUS HUMANA

Wolves are intelligent creatures,
Just like humans too.
They need packs to survive,
But some don't know who to go to.

They won't ever give up,
They carry on exploring.
Until they find 'the one',
And that sounds luring.

Wait. Who is that over there...
With that gorgeous fur?
Do I dare?
Will she care?

Humans are romantic creatures,
Just like wolves too.
They need love to survive,
Just like me and you.

This is the end of the story,
Where two lovers meet.
Lupus and Humana.
And may their hearts forever beat.

Jack George Baker (14)
Beaumont Leys School, Leicester

BABY BLUE

The vivid icy sea was moving slowly,
The bright blue sky sparkled above me.
Children laughing on the beach, playing in the sea.
Sound of waves hitting the rocks in front of me.
The scent of ice cream was delicious
As it hovered in the air.
I really do love it in Cornwall!

Ella Harvey (11)
Beaumont Leys School, Leicester

DEAR FUTURE LIFE

Don't worry about a thing,
Live and learn but don't waste time,
Working hard will pay off!

You only have one family,
So be careful on what you say,
Be a nice person.

Don't judge a book by its cover,
They might be a genuine person,
So give them a chance.

The stars are the limit,
Never give up in life,
Even if things are hard.

Wear what you want,
Ignore all the haters,
It's your choice not theirs.

Dance like nobody's watching,
Because you only have one life,
So do not waste it.

Nadine Dorset (11)
Beaumont Leys School, Leicester

FOOTBALL MATCH!

Excited supporters cheering us on.
Players sprinting backwards and forwards,
Backwards and forwards.
Managers calling simple instructions.
Screaming and shouting – screaming and shouting,
When the opposition scores.
Wet sweat from the players.
Bisto from the food vans.
The nerves when I walk on the pitch.
This is what football is all about.

Jack Fitches (12)
Beaumont Leys School, Leicester

DEAR FUTURE SELF

Here is some advice
To always be nice to others
And never be so bad.

Always be yourself
In front of anyone
No matter how mean.

Always enjoy life
Even when it brings you down
Always bring love and smiles.

Never be afraid
Because there is always good
Behind the corner.

Don't be friends with bad
Always make a connection,
To those who are good.

Just achieve your dreams
And love your family fully
'Cause you are who you are.

Shruti Patel (11)
Beaumont Leys School, Leicester

DEAR FUTURE SELF

Hope I get a family
I hope I get a good job
Hope I get a house.

I hope I have a baby
A girl not a boy
I hope I get a car.

Hope I stay out of bad trouble
Hope I have done good
Never give up, be yourself.

Ella Pallett (11)
Beaumont Leys School, Leicester

DEAR FUTURE SELF

Do not doubt yourself
You can be anything you want
Just believe in yourself.

Be kind to your parents
Soon you will be by yourself
Always have faith every day.

Be happy and kind
Be loving and gentle to all
Always be happy.

Don't care about looks
Do something you will enjoy
Be happy and kind.

Try hard at school
Go to university
Be joyful and kind.

Life is too short
Don't care what people think
Life doesn't grow on trees.

Avva Shaboull (11)
Beaumont Leys School, Leicester

DEAR FUTURE SELF

Hi Brodie Potter,
Have you got a motorbike?
I hope so.

First, pass your exams
So that you can get a job,
Earn money, get a bike!

Blue, fast, fantastic,
You could buy one for a Christmas present
Just for you.

Brodie Potter (11)
Beaumont Leys School, Leicester

DEAR FUTURE SELF

Never give up, try,
Because you only have one life,
So live it happily.

Forgive and forget,
You only have one family,
So think before you say.

Hard work will pay,
Get the best education,
Do not doubt yourself.

You only have one chance,
Live it to the fullest,
Be a nice person.

Be original, be happy, be different,
Dance like nobody's watching,
Don't change who you are.

Remember always smile,
Do anything that scares you,
Succeed and be happy!

Alicia Chauhan (11)
Beaumont Leys School, Leicester

DEAR FUTURE SELF

Here is what I'll say
To you my dear future self
From me, your school past.

My advice to you
Be yourself always and be
kind and caring too.

Don't ever worry
I hope you liked the story
What will be will be.

Weronika Gistinger (11)
Beaumont Leys School, Leicester

DEAR FUTURE SELF

Something you should know -
I want to know if I'll grow.
How tall will I be?

So listen to this poem,
You may just want to know it.
Repeat after me.

Be a nice person,
Be kind, thoughtful and caring.
What will be will be!

Do I have a car?
Will I have my own new house?
Love life – it's worth it!

Spend on things you need.
Save your money carefully.
Not the opposite.

Look forwards, not back.
Be prepared for what's to come.
Do not have regrets!

Tilly Derry (11)
Beaumont Leys School, Leicester

HELL

Torturous lava jumping out of nowhere.
Fireball coming from the Ghost of Hell,
Blowing up everything.

Terrifying ghastly screams,
Unusual steps of Zombie pigmen.

The sulphur smell of warts,
The bitter taste of potions.

Eternal suffering.

Josh Thanki (12)
Beaumont Leys School, Leicester

DEAR FUTURE SELF

Here is some advice,
To live longer in this life,
From Sally to me.

Love yourself for you
Have eight children at home,
Fall deeply in love.

Listen to others,
Live your life fabulously,
Love your family.

Travel the whole world,
Get to explore new cultures,
Live to the fullest.

Be a great mother,
Make life last before it ends,
Don't rush too quickly.

Think beyond your skills,
When it's almost time to end,
You have been a star.

Salimatu Kin (11)
Beaumont Leys School, Leicester

ICE CREAM

I could eat you for breakfast,
Or in the red-hot sun.
You have the best tasting flavours
That go yum in my tum.
When it starts to get hot
You'll melt, so eat me fast
Otherwise I won't last.
My volcanic strawberry-flavoured ice cream
Tastes yummy in my tummy.

Daley Blasdale-Moore
Beaumont Leys School, Leicester

MONEY

When all of your hope hangs in a 2%
You set out on a mission to find out where the other 98 went.
It lies in the hands of something sweet as honey,
As dangerous as fire, of course it's money.
It brings you up and takes you down,
It will buy you a fancy house in town.
It will destroy your life if you don't have enough,
You'll leave your wife when the getting is tough.
You can buy things with it that are illegal without fail,
But don't worry, if you have enough it can get you out of jail.
It can make you look pretty when you're really not,
It can get you out of winter and to a tropical spot.
It can save you and give you an education,
It can get you out of a sticky situation.
It can buy fake affections and desires,
It can rebuild things destroyed by fires.
But unfortunately for some, it has no effect on people who are real.
People who have extreme emotions and can actually feel
To keep people in my life forever I would give my every penny
But honestly, I don't think I have that many.

Punit Patel (14)
Beaumont Leys School, Leicester

THE HAUNTED HOUSE

Run! Run! Run! From the red-eyed monster chasing me through the halls.
Bumping into knotty cobwebs that cover the walls.
There is banging on the wall.
The quiet tap of spiders crawling across the floor.
A strong odour of rotting bodies is in the air giving me a scare
And the stench of Hell makes me fall into an old rocking chair.
Tonight we're in the haunted house
And all I feel is dead.

Katie Hickenbotham (11)
Beaumont Leys School, Leicester

DEAR FUTURE SELF

Forget the past
And look to the future,
You have one life so live it.

Be kind to your parents
As they do anything
And everything for you.

Live and learn and achieve.
Learn for seven, enjoy for thirty.
This is how life works.

Don't judge a book by its cover
And don't doubt yourself.
Just work hard and play hard.

Cherish your work
And it will pay off.
Love life and enjoy life.

Be positive
Or the negativity will overcome you.

Dhilan Rupen Nakum (11)
Beaumont Leys School, Leicester

DEAR FUTURE SELF

Here is some advice
Please don't dye your hair.
Live life! Love life! Enjoy life!
Love the way you are.

Please don't have any children
Respect the elders
Try hard in GCSEs.

How tall are you now?
Forget negative people
Always look the best.

Caitlin Fletcher (11)
Beaumont Leys School, Leicester

DEAR FUTURE SELF

Here is some advice,
Be as strong as you can be,
Don't be a woosy.

Be a good person,
Have an amazing future,
Always be yourself.

Be a fashion girl,
Get a ticket to Paris,
Be wild and free.

Buy a fashionable house,
Make dresses for a living,
Earn money by it.

Live long, get married,
It's all about fashion now,
Live long, live well, bye.

Jamie-Leigh Mewis (11)
Beaumont Leys School, Leicester

DEAR FUTURE SELF

Live life to the fullest,
Have as much fun as you want.
Be nice to people.

Be kind and thoughtful;
Every choice you made was one,
Bring love and smiles.

Stop all the worry,
Don't argue with your parents,
We're no invisible.

Don't have regrets,
It is silly and pointless,
You just never know.

Amar Naliyapara (11)
Beaumont Leys School, Leicester

DEAR FUTURE SELF

Here is some advice
About my future life
So please listen to me.

Stop all the worry
It's pointless and unhealthy
Life is very short.

Be kind to people
Bring happiness to the world
Life is a big smile.

Live all your dreams because
You'll regret it if you don't
Live it, don't dream it.

I hope this will help
The rest is up to you now
What will be will be!

Demirra Green (11)
Beaumont Leys School, Leicester

DEAR FUTURE SELF

Be good all your life
I hope you understand
Don't commit a crime.

Get good grades at school
Get a satisfying job
All well and all good.

I hope you agree
That life is in your hands
Make exciting good plans.

Here is some advice
I hope you live all your life
From me to myself.

Alex Frith (11)
Beaumont Leys School, Leicester

DEAR FUTURE SELF

I'm writing to me,
Live life to the fullest,
Live, laugh, cry and love.

Don't be negative,
Always have a go and try
And never give up.

Do I become rich?
Do I achieve my life goals?
Do I get my job?

Are there flying cars?
Is there still McDonald's?
Is there World War Three?

Well, until next time,
I hope you reply back,
Can't wait to be you.

Niam Raval (11)
Beaumont Leys School, Leicester

DEAR FUTURE SELF

Please listen to me
I hope I will be like this
From me to myself.

Please be nice to people
Always think about your actions
Try to get a job.

Live a very happy life
Live your dreams and don't hold back please
Do not have regrets.

This is some advice
For my future life, be good
I hope you understand.

Jacob Canham (11)
Beaumont Leys School, Leicester

FEELINGS

Happy, sad, we all have feelings
Sometimes high, sometimes low
Nobody likes to let them show.
Laughing when I'm happy is such a joy
My mum was shocked when she had a boy!

My dad was sad when his team lost
He started moaning when he saw the cost.
The trainers were the best I could find
My best friend is very kind.

I got so angry that day in May
I had a cold which wouldn't go away.
I screamed and shouted all day long
I couldn't sing my favourite song.

Happy or sad we know how it feels
Like breaking a pair of high heels.

Georgia Elizabeth Pattison (12)
Beaumont Leys School, Leicester

FOXY THE FOX PIRATE

As soon as I went to visit Freddy Fazbear and friends
The only one I was attracted to was Foxy,
The way he looked fell into me,
His pirate voice put me in a trance,
All I needed was one single glance – *boom!*
His muscular figure and his strong legs made me more obsessed,
But his fluffy handsome face drawing me in,
Made me fall in love with him and his horrible hook,
Not just impression but also words,
Led me to a whole new world,
When he waves his hook to say hello,
I always know he is my beau
And I'm his Bae ... Mangle!

Amber Green (12)
Beaumont Leys School, Leicester

A WAR ZONE

As I run through the trees,
With my team in our ghillie suits,
Rifle in hand, hunting for foe,
Tripping over tree roots in our big heavy boots;
Too many tracks to follow,
Which way do we go?
We hear the sound of a rifle shot.
One of my fellow soldiers falls to the ground,
We all turn and gaze in fear,
Looking around my heart starts to pound.
I suddenly feel the pain and a ringing in my ear.
I find I've been shot by a massive . . . pink . . . paintball . . .
We all walk away in paint-splattered glory!

Ella Basavci (12)
Beaumont Leys School, Leicester

SYLVIA

The 13th of August felt so long,
Since you left us and you were gone.
You closed your eyes for the final time,
I remember Mum broke down and she cried.
We were crying, in so much pain,
To know that we would never see you again.

Your dancing, your singing is gravely missed,
You were full of so much happiness.
You did like to drink tea.
You really do mean everything to me.
You are my guardian angel above.
I will never forget your eternal love.

Amy Walton
Beaumont Leys School, Leicester

DEAR FUTURE SELF

Always be yourself,
Forget all the nasty things,
Don't change yourself.

Stay the way you are,
Take care of your parents,
Keep the good things.

Explore yourself,
Do the most scary things,
Don't do the wrong things.

Forget your mistakes,
Be nice to your brother,
Make up with old friends.

Make some new friends,
Do the job you want to do.
Be free with yourself.

Always be yourself.
Forget all the nasty things.
Don't change yourself.

Stay the way you are.

Alfie Cronin (11)
Beaumont Leys School, Leicester

SOCIAL MOBILITY

You placed on a mountain
And I held by ground, doubting
Whether to climb and conquer or to subside silently.

I build my ladder from hard work
Whereas you buy one with wealth.
When I try and reach for the sky,
You've already got the shining and shimmering stars.

The cruel kindness that was marked on us by blood,
They label us by birth
As plucking a rose bud
Because one day the rose will become earth.

Manna Blesson
Beaumont Leys School, Leicester

RONALDO

Ronaldo, a young star,
A Portuguese prince
Heading towards the ball,
He's been playing football ever since.

Floating towards the ball,
In control,
Knowing what to do next,
He's on a roll.

So there you go England,
Rooney's on a yellow,
Let's see you try to beat us,
'Cause Ronaldo's the fellow.

Portugal will win,
Just you see,
We are the best,
It's meant to be.

Hummaad Badat (11)
Eden Boys Preston, Preston

LOVING AND KIND – YOUR BEAUTIFUL MOTHER

Every day she's awake, just
For me she's so loving and kind,
my mother,
Yet I don't appreciate it,
All I say is thank you,
I don't say I love you
Or you're the best mother in the world,
I just say thank you,
She loves me with all her heart
Yet I love her with half my heart.
The night I left her,
She wept and wept
And I showed no sorrow or mercy
And then I returned to get my belongings, I didn't say anything and
then stormed out and I left her with my sister,
No one there to comfort her
Except my sister two years later.
I missed her,
I regretted the fact I left her
But it was too late.
'She died,' my sister said,
'It was all your fault.'
I lived regretting every moment of my life,
All I could remember was how loving
And kind she was – my mother,
so kids never diss or hate your mother,
Remember she loves you,
So love her back and don't make the same mistake I did.
Just love your family.

Hamza Harun Patel (11)
Eden Boys Preston, Preston

MUHAMMED (PBUH) PROPHET

He came to this world to preach and teach
He has never committed a sin
He was a great leader
He even respects a little creature
He was the best
Better than the rest
He was kind
Caring
Careful
Safe
Jolly
Happy
Equal
Helpful
Loving
Friendly
Truthful
Successful
Honest
He would show modesty
Fairness
Kindness
Respectfulness
Compassion
Special
Well-behaved
Humble
Nice
Thoughtful.

Abdur-Rahmaan Adam (11)
Eden Boys Preston, Preston

MESSI THE BEST

Messi, the best player for sure
The best footballer,
He will always try hard
And win the Ballon d'Or

He has players around
To help him score goals,
He is so good,
He makes people fall.

He runs past everyone
Like they are not there,
The opponents say to themselves,
'That's not fair!'

He's a leader
And offering lessons in football,
He has something different
To anyone in the world.

Messi's kick takes control of every soul,
Even his enemies celebrate the goals.
His sublime kick stuns many on the bench,
Even King Pelé can't help but nod his head.

Messi's not an ordinary star,
He's an iconic figure.
I call him a modern day art,
Gracing each and every soccer fixture.

Faizan Patel (11)
Eden Boys Preston, Preston

THE POETRY TRIALS - FUTURE VOICES

MY ROLE MODEL

He is humble
He is kind
He is a guide
He is noble
My messenger
My prophet
Muhammad
Muhammad
I love him with all my heart
I admire him with my soul
Muhammad
Muhammad
He is trustworthy
He is truthful
He is a leader
He is my rapid cheetah
Muhammad
Muhammad
He preached the religion Islam
He worshipped the one god
He never killed anyone in battle
He only scathed someone in war
Muhammad
Muhammad
My role model.

Khubaib Patel (11)
Eden Boys Preston, Preston

THE MAZE

As I walked in
I saw a large griffin
The maze stretched for miles
It had many paths
As I started to walk
I had to stop
To choose which way to go
Right or left
I went straight ahead
A big space appeared
Where there were lots of spears
As I picked one up
It led me in the right direction
It pulled
And pulled
And pulled
Until it stopped
There it was
The end of the maze
Had finally come
Playing this game
Had been so much fun
Writing this poem
My story had finally been done.

Ali Ahmad (11)
Eden Boys Preston, Preston

RONALDO

You are my inspiration
You are the light of football
You are strong
You are famous
You are rich
You are out of this world.

You skill players with ease
You nutmeg them
You roulette them
You rainbow flick them
You dribble past them.

You score amazing goals
Bottom left corner
Bottom right corner
Top right corner
Top left corner
Post and in
Crossbar and in.

You help the poor
You sold your golden boot
And gave the money to the poor
Can I be like you?

Zayd Ahmed (11)
Eden Boys Preston, Preston

FEAR

The sound of fear swept through the air
It sounded like a grizzly bear
Who is this monster so big and grey
Where does it come from and what is its prey?

Its gigantic arms and hairy legs
Smelt of fish and rotten eggs
Its tummy was extremely fat
Its arms swung like a cricket bat.

Its head was round, as round as could be
His tiny eyes I could hardly see
Its green teeth were long and sharp
And his tongue was short and dark.

His nails were dirty and brown
The edge of it was pointing down
His toes were repulsive and black
He likes to catch people and throw them in a sack.

Where do we run to, where do we hide?
How do we escape his fearsome glide?
A place of safety and serenity we seek
A place where no fear will peek.

Khalid Bapu (11)
Eden Boys Preston, Preston

FOOTBALL FRENZY

I have always liked football.
Such a rough game.
Such skills and speed are required.

Football is the start of it all.
Home town watching on Sunday morning.

When one day I found that I needed to withdraw,
It was the honourable thing to do.

Ubaydullah Shahbaz (12)
Eden Boys Preston, Preston

WHY I ADMIRE MY FATHER?

He is my father
but he is also my friend.
He is always there for me
and always ready to help.

He is very smart and clever
just like his father too.
Both are good with business
and both love their families too.

He likes to be a kid sometimes
but he is also very strict.
I have three sisters and two brothers
and he treats us all equally.

My father is very cool and kind,
he taught me to be respectful to all of mankind.
My father taught me everything I know
I want him to know that I love him more.

God combined all these qualities
And then completed his masterpiece.
Some people call him Father
but I call him my dad.

Muhammad Isap (11)
Eden Boys Preston, Preston

HAPPY POEM

A happy day that has a heart,
Full of happiness every day.
A happy boy has a big smile every day.

The happy boy never looks back
At the things that make him sad.

The happy boy always looks back
At the things that made him happy.

Mohammad Patel (10)
Eden Boys Preston, Preston

THE PROPHET (SAW)

I am writing a poem
So I don't know where you're going.
Please stay,
There must be a way.
I'm talking about the prophet,
Who never said, 'Stop it.'
He had a very good mind
For the whole of mankind.
He decreased badness
He increased goodness
He was sent to the Cave of Heerah
A message sent by Allah.
He was a beloved man
That people never ran.
He went to Makkah
Where they placed the Kaaba.
He was born in Makkah
He passed away peacefully in Madeenah
His mother was Aminah.
So I hope you enjoy my poem,
Now, you'd better get going!

Taahir Wadee (11)
Eden Boys Preston, Preston

MY DAD

My dad is the best,
He's the best out of all the rest.
When he's mad he writes in his pad.
He's a big lad
And when I'm sad he gives me a pat.
He sends me to a school.
I hated every minute of learning but I didn't quit
Because of my dad.
Then I lived myself as a champion.

Yousaf Mohammad (11)
Eden Boys Preston, Preston

SCARED

Strong but weak
Happy but then sad
Sometimes feeling hopeful
Always dreading the bad.

Scared and uncertain
Where will it end?
Way too frightened
Too peer past the bend.

Why has life dealt me
This terrible blow?
I used to feel great
But now I feel low.

I feel so frustrated
And angry, unsure
Will I ever experience
Life again as before.

Muhammad Muzzammil Irfan Dhanna (11)
Eden Boys Preston, Preston

BIRD

Soaring through the sky,
Amongst all the fields,
Giving a little cry
And so did the seagulls.

Feeling all my feathers,
Looking at the grass,
Smelling fresh flowers,
All of them I pass.

It's time for me to pray,
Because it's the end of the day,
We all circle round
And create a sound.

Mohammed Vohra (11)
Eden Boys Preston, Preston

MY MUM AND DAD

My mum is the best
She's better than the rest
When my room is a mess
She tidies it up for me
Then she makes me a lovely cup of tea
My mum is the best
Better than the rest.

My dad is a great big lad
When I make him really mad
He writes in his pad
That I've been very bad
But he never shouts at me
My dad is the best
Better than the rest.

Aanish Mohammad (12)
Eden Boys Preston, Preston

FIRST LEGEND

Flabbergasted
Exicted
Proud
I was.

I told my brother
He was shocked
Mad
Happy.

I boasted like a lion
Who killed its first zebra.

I hugged my mum
Cos I got legendary
Randy Orton.

Sakil Patel (11)
Eden Boys Preston, Preston

THE BELIEVER

My hands, they shake with sorrow,
Making me want to borrow,
My lonely heart bleeding with pain,
Making me feel like a man in chains,
My soul forever wishing me to have stayed,
Making me feel that I can change my ways,
My mind was saying, 'You can definitely change your ways.'
My money could help the poor,
My character could guide people to the right door,
My eyesight could help the blind,
My kindness could help the ones who have been declined,
My fellow brothers remember we are a big family,
That help towards making us all a happy society.

Ebrahim Gangat (11)
Eden Boys Preston, Preston

WEATHER MONSTER

Having tea like dogs licking their supper
The light goes off in a thud, only the moonlight to protect them.

The thunder loud as a crowd of people, a shock.
Birds howling like wolves being afraid.

Flaring candles like snow, clouds whistling
And windows screaming, children's eyes glooming
With tears
And
The
Moonlight
Staring at us.

Hanzalah Ukadia (11)
Eden Boys Preston, Preston

MY MOTHER

My mum is the best
Better than the rest
She wakes me up for school
She is really cool.

She makes yummy food
And is always in a happy mood.
My favourite food is pizza and chips
and some tasty dips.

When I am not well
She looks after me
She comforts me
Until I recover.

My mum always lets me go where I want,
Like Blackpool or the park,
Playing with friends
Or going to the beach.

My mum is amazing!

Zaid Bagia (12)
Eden Boys Preston, Preston

THEIR FUTURES

The battle is won but the child is lost,
Humans are evolving, but at what cost?
'Ring-a-ring o' roses, a pocketful of posies,'
Echoes in your mind, just to keep you the same,
Everyone says, 'It wasn't your fault!' Then who was to blame?
The distress kicks in, what is the poor girl in?
Scary thoughts grow in your mind,
Have they made her deaf, perhaps maybe blind?
You spin a night terror, all in your head,
As you toss and turn in your creaking bed.
Then . . . sunrise, you grieve for your loss,
As the church bell chimes, shaking the tower's moss,
But what about their futures, do they walk free?
Whilst your girl's dead, what do they start to be?

Callum Fradley (13)
Endon High School, Stoke-On-Trent

TOMORROW

In the back of a police car with my head spinnin',
Was it really worth those days of pure bingeing?
Looking back on all the stuff I did without reason,
Tomorrow I need to stand up in front of a judge and start pleading,
The thought of it makes my heart start beating.

Was it really worth it?
Getting in a state,
Being sick on a copper's shoes,
Not worth a litre of cider and that box of blues.
Hopefully tomorrow I'll have some good news,
I want this children's home to be my last move.

Aidan Darragh Donnan (15)
Groomsport Intensive Support Unit, Bangor

MY POEM ABOUT LIGHT!

Spitting out their gum,
Chanting and shouting very loud,
Under the dim lights,
Suddenly ear-piercing screams,
Bring you down onto
Your knees, your head starts to bleed,
The blood trickles down,
As you fall to the hard ground,
The light flickers out . . .

Isobella Frudd
Hodgson Academy, Poulton-Le-Fylde

THE MODERN PUPPET

A man he came
He picked up the game
He brought me fame
Committed crimes under my name
Making me roam
Right into a home
But hey, I've got a car made with chrome
Hit it into a dome
Forced me to go quick and far
Broke my 10th car
A voice in my head, I'm going around the bend
Oh dear God make it end
'OK now Fred, go to bed'
Now get a bit of time until I watch blood red.

Cameron Bishop (14)
Kettlebrook Short Stay School, Tamworth

THE POETRY TRIALS - FUTURE VOICES

LOVE

Love is sometimes enlightening
It shines bright in our lives
It comes like bolts of lightning
It will see you through the worst times

But love will sometimes hurt
It will burn you deep inside
It could turn your glee to dirt
It might cut you to the core

Love is sometimes good
Sometimes terrible
But it will forever be deciding our future.

Bethany Lewis (14)
Kettlebrook Short Stay School, Tamworth

I LOVE BOOKS!

I can read a book in a day,
They make me want to shout, 'Hooray!'
I like every genre and every type,
I even read them to friends on Skype.
I don't mind reading a school book,
Because they leave me totally hooked.
Sometimes I stay up all night,
But books just fill me with delight.
When I go to the library at school,
I feel lost in my own forest of cool.
I read books at break and lunch,
Even though I miss out on all the food to munch.
I even consider writing my own,
I've typed some ideas up on my phone.
Books are incredible, books are great,
Read one now and please don't wait!

Elizabeth Dewes (11)
Kings Norton Girls School, Birmingham

HE MADE ME ROT

He made me rot from the outside in.

With his sour breath
and cold strong hands that felt like death
that pinned me down
as his body buried mine into the ground

I scratched scars on my chest.
They look like slugs and feel as slimy as his tongue does
But
I needed to find my heart and squeeze it into a
different rhythm than the one that he left me with.

And at night, I cry on my back so my tears
trail as worms straight to my ears,
so I can remember his words:

You have to admit, that felt good though, right?

It does not feel good to rot.

I could not run in case somebody caught me.
I could not eat because I couldn't taste anything but him in my throat.

I would not smile
And I pulled out my hair
And I carved lines on my face trying to look fierce so
No one would ever come near me again.

My muscles died,
My stomach shrivelled,
My skin peeled off.

I started to rot
But it felt better than he did.

Flora Slorach (17)
Kings Norton Girls School, Birmingham

MY BESTIE

My best friend Emma Wilson
You're my bestie pie
I've got your back, and you've got mine,
We're each other's Valentines
To see you hurt, to see you cry
It makes me weep and want to die
We have so many memories
That will never say goodbye
We share all our secrets
And never tell a lie,
We share every heartbreak
And every breath we take
And if you agree to never fight
It doesn't matter, who's wrong or right
Hand in hand, love is sent
We'll be besties till the end!

Sophie Marshall (14)
King's Park Secondary School, Glasgow

FEAR

It's just because
I look different
That's why you're all scared of me
You can only see what's wrong with me
And not what's right.
Don't you think if I could change it I would?
Don't you think I know how?
I know I am hard to look at,
I don't even like looking at myself.
If I could break every mirror
I'd break it into a thousand pieces.

Susan Jamieson (13)
King's Park Secondary School, Glasgow

MUSIC FROM THE HEART

Bows rising falling
Singing out a tune of joy
Songs from old times past.

Francesca Clayton (15)
Kirkstone House School, Peterborough

THE LADY OF THE SEA

On the sandy beach the waters lie
Children and mothers running by
Heat is blooming as sun fills the sky
Yet one young lady alone and shy
The rushing of the sea
She sits alone on the water's side
Likening to the waves in them she sighed
No one to talk to or confide
The lady of the sea.

Watching as time passes the clock
Waiting for her lover's boat to dock
Raising her soul with the twist of a lock
Yet her husband's boat still out at rock
The silence of the sea
Years have been, yet there she remains
Sitting on the rock like tied with chains
But refusing to leave for her heart it pains
The lady of the sea.

No one sees her, yet she's always there
Skin is pale and hair so fair
Her clothes are perfection yet simple and bare
Shining off her is the ocean's glare
The shimmer of the sea
A century ago her lover left the key
He was exploring and sailing on order of decree
Yet before he went he said to thee,
'Wait for me my love, you're my lady of the sea.'

Ffion Rogers (15)
Les Beaucamps High School, Guernsey

AN ABANDONED FARM

Through my window I see no star,
I see a much closer mysterious farm.
Horses live and sleep,
But I don't know who crosses the deep.

Someone or something must live there.
But all the public know,
There is a gap where the wind blows.

The place is silent and unaware.

The farm is like a part of a patchwork quilt,
The barn is one of the many stone houses built.
The sky is clear,
While I see a deer.

Through my window I see no star,
I see a much closer mysterious farm.

Katie Hazel
Lightcliffe Academy, Halifax

THE PROBLEM (ADHD)

People try to fix me
But failed so far
All I want is to be free
Everything is so confusing, so bizarre

It's like living with another you
You wouldn't understand
It's never left or changed even though I grew
I'm lost and alone on a never-ending land

The problem grabs me and never lets go
The depression and emptiness, it's all too much
The problem is not a friend more like a foe
It's a feeling no one else can touch

Sometimes I feel constricted
Like a snake wound round a tree
I don't feel alive, I feel restricted
How can they understand, I want to be free

The doctors give me meds to try and help
They don't really listen to what I have to say
At the end of the day I could cry and yelp
My life is broken on repeat, but now it's a new day

People try to fix 'it'
But it's failing so far
I can rise up and take over 'it'
I now feel myself floating, explosive like a star.

Sean Robson (15)
Moorbridge PRU, Newcastle Upon Tyne

SHIELDS OF THE GILL

I am the sea,
The wailing waves over the harsh breeze.
Starlight and moonrise
with drowned droplets for eyes.
A darkened light in the range.
The gradient. As am I;
A change.
Paralysed in midwave stage.

As the mechanical wings of my turbines unfurl,
Welcoming to the dungeons of the Underworld.
A tunnelled wasteland of decay and debris.
A broken connection of rivers and streams.
I am not; I am the sea.

Forgive my solidity, impenetrable and felicity.
Cowering in the midst oblivion of my scrutiny.

I'm hostile, and I'm shattered; a fighter, a defender ...
But it's the man on his feet on the verge of surrender.
Listen! Listen! Can't you hear the impending doom?
It's shaking under your gills; the claustrophobia in the room.
Oh, but still, your ignorance is the cure.
Never mind, old friend, for it can follow you to shore.
Spawns a swarm of stampeding swords.
The one with none but a chance to fall.

Though mind my friction plates of habit.
Cause a sinful storm inside my core and burrow like a rabbit.

Are you waiting for me, my love? I told you not to stay!
Run to warm while I take my form and leave my corpse where it lay.

I am the sea, a beast without a leash.
Solidity, felicity.
Sea, I see.

Deanna Dawkins (17)
New College, Swindon

THE POETRY TRIALS - FUTURE VOICES

NOT ALL THAT GLITTERS IS GOOD

Divinity?

Let me tell you something about divinity.

Divinity is spilled blood and black ink,
both staining old parchment in the name of a Holy Father.
It's angels swearing that they are good,
(even as they raise their swords up against their own siblings).
It's golden stardust seeping into the universe, out of black holes and constellations,
changing,
changing,
changing.

Divinity is stained swords and red apples,
split lips and broken bones.
It's angels fighting wars that have long since ended,
carrying the weight of worlds in their hands,
and pretending everything is fine.
Divinity isn't white.
It's gold and blood-red, ancient and unforgiving.
Say it's in the name of your Father, young one.
Say it is pure.

Divinity is a puddle sinking into the earth, spreading and stretching.
It's clear water finding blood and taking it in.
It's beasts baring teeth with flesh in between.
It's tainting souls and grace in shards.
Divinity has not been good for centuries.
Divinity has been broken, my love.

So next time you call for something divine,
remember, remember,
that divinity is dangerous,
and angels are not to be trusted.

Leandra Inglis (17)
New College, Swindon

NIGHT

The sun has kept its soul unattended
on this God-given day, spoon-fed
'til it bled crimson gold and
scorching sand that is cold.

The trees have taken a forbidden shade
and the geometric pavements closed in
on themselves, dried out, pruned up
come undone, come down, come out.

The moon has come out
and the clouds mourn for the stars
as they wait six hours for the sun
to come back and confront the dead of night
and let it speak one last time.

'Come in,' said Night
'Let's not fight,' it cried
and the blood orange on its hands has now dried
and it lied to Sun's face, wretched Night
as it reached to eternally shut off the light.

And, no, I don't trust the dead of night
because it is dead
there is not a fraction of light
the friction makes me so damn blind.

'Wretched night so dead,'
I said as I lied my head
and reached for the lamp
sparking up the neon sun
Night Night
Goodbye
Kiss Kiss.

Jonatan Akala (16)
New College, Swindon

LIGHT THE FIRE

Burn the buildings, let the ashes scatter,
Let the flames turn everything to matter,
Hear the screams of the children,
Hurry the firemen, blurred vision.

Let the water dance to calm the anger,
Don't let the flames erupt with amber,
Keep the children away from the mess,
Or else the leader shall confess.

My child was my whole, my life, my soul,
One day she took a stroll,
Not once has she said goodbye, lonely as me;
I thought she loved me, but then she had to flee.

Why cause the damage?
The lives of the human race burn in rampage,
Though you hear screams,
The fire doesn't give, because she is so mean.

The flame that used to be alight,
Is now as dead as night,
But once that flame ignites once more;
Shall the fire begin again, let the children uproar.

Liz Malihan (16)
New College, Swindon

WHO AM I?

'I am the one who cries,' says the silhouette,
Who exists in the light.

'I am the one who dreams,' the light proclaims,
Keeping darkness at bay.

The memories sighed, 'We are the ones who live in the past,
Never to move forward.'

The lips stayed motionless as ears listen,
They are progression, ready to adapt.

'I am a mess,' I say,
'A mind fragmented,

Split in two by the actions of others
But I am healing, repairing.'

Shannon Nicole Harwood (18)
New College, Swindon

SINKING

You start at the top,
Then slowly you sink,
And you can't stop.

It gives you time to think,
As you dive to the deep abyss,
You could even rethink.

The silence could be bliss,
There's no going back,
There's no getting out of this.

Your surroundings turn pitch-black,
As you keep falling,
Through the sea wreck.

As you sink into the dreaded sea,
Wishing once again to be free.

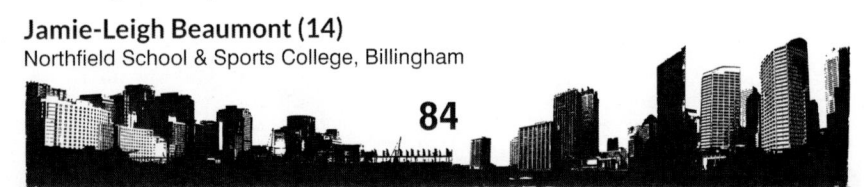

Jamie-Leigh Beaumont (14)
Northfield School & Sports College, Billingham

THE POETRY TRIALS - FUTURE VOICES

SHE WHO SPEAKS TO NONE

I have one feature less
Than most, upon my recluse face.
Eye, eye, nose, that's all I need
To compete in the daily rat race,
Because she who speaks to none,
Has opinions no one wants,
Doesn't need a mouth.

My words are irrelevant to everyone,
Bully or so-called friend,
So to stop the hurt and knocking down,
I will stay quiet until the end,
Because she who speaks to none,
Has opinions no one wants,
Doesn't have a mouth.

Silence makes you isolated, but it's
The easiest way to be,
Answer no questions, say no words
And the bullies don't notice me,
Because she who speaks to none,
Has opinions no one wants,
Doesn't want a mouth.

My thoughts are my only company,
I live a pretty desolate life,
But it's the price you pay
To not be bullied and to stay out of the schoolyard strife,
Because she who speaks to none,
Has opinions no one wants,
Is lonely.

Holly Dobbing (13)
Northfield School & Sports College, Billingham

SMILES TO GIVE

So many things said and done
that make you feel different ways.

Through thick and thin just note
someone's always on the same page.

And you may think no one wants
to listen to what you have to say.

But everyone's got ears and hands
to wipe those tears away.

However, how many people does
it take to make some realise

That what they say is not just
words but in their hands our lives?

Now you might think that what
you say the people know is lies

But do they, or underneath is
there something that they hide?

Now you need to know that it's
up to yourself and we don't choose for you.

But you are not alone, no one's ever
alone and there's always someone there for you.

Always note that there are so
many reasons and lots of good times to live.

So never let them beat you
and show you've still got smiles to give.

Lucy Stubbs (14)
Northfield School & Sports College, Billingham

LONELINESS

I watch them having fun,
Making friends, making memories.
It aches to know.
I can't do that.
I am too scared.
It traps me here, frozen to the spot.
My arms go rigid, and my lungs feel like they fill up with ice.
My head is numb. I can't breathe.

It hurts me to feel.
The pain this all puts me through.
I have no memories.

When I turn away,
I will myself to turn back
But the pain is too strong.

You see, I had friends once
But they hurt me
And left me alone.
I cannot have friends, they always hurt me
So I stay here, hurting, crying, watching.
I am stuck here, unmoving, rigid.
They know what they have done.

I'm broken.

Lucy Cossavella (13)
Northfield School & Sports College, Billingham

SORROW

I sit waiting in my chair,
Aching muscles,
Sore nose,
Itchy throat,
A far bittering cold.

I sit patiently with no obligation,
With no intention,
With no doubt that I was forgotten.

I sit unoccupied with only this poem,
Nothing else but the dark gloom of the night,
No one dares to look at me,
Nor talk or communicate.

I sit listening and hearing them talking amongst themselves,
Mention my name over and over
But never would they bear an eye,
Am I forgotten or just ignored?
Either way I still sit in my gloom.

However, there is a possibility they will look
But at the moment, I sit forgotten.

Niall Watson (13)
Northfield School & Sports College, Billingham

LONELINESS

Being lonely doesn't
Mean having nobody next to you.
Being lonely doesn't
Mean not having anyone to love.
Being lonely doesn't
Mean you don't have people surrounding you.
Being lonely means
Seeing the one you love the most forget you
And love someone else.

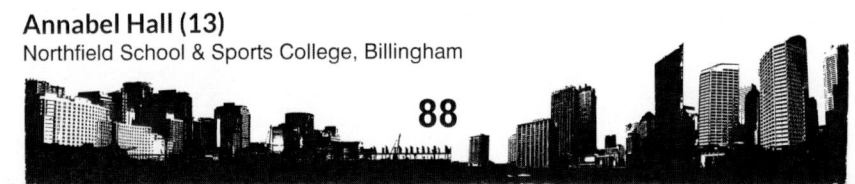

Annabel Hall (13)
Northfield School & Sports College, Billingham

A LONELY LIFE

As darkness fills the space of my mind,
As the dark twisted way of life unwinds.
The men around me are never kind,
I look for comfort but it's the one thing I cannot find.

I feel alone out here,
Like a dark cloud on a tranquil blue day.
There's nothing here for me and yet I stay
I don't know why.
I guess it's because it's the only way.

Day and night I work
Surrounded by shadows,
Only moving never speaking,
There's no one to talk to, nobody who cares
I don't know how much longer I can bear.

I am a prisoner here,
I feel trapped in a cage,
But the cage is my mind
And I can't escape . . .

Emma Shears (13)
Northfield School & Sports College, Billingham

DESPAIR

Behind the smile, we can see the tears
Inside our hearts, we feel the fears
Behind the strength, we can see your despair
Inside our souls, we feel that isn't fair
Inside your eyes, we see the broken dreams
I know how desperate it all seems
In your voice, we can hear your pain
I know you're struggling to stay sane
Listen to our words: we care for you
Giving up on you is something I'll never do.

Stephanie Otterson (13)
Northfield School & Sports College, Billingham

GONE FOREVER

I miss the times when you were here
Protecting me from all of the fear.
Helping me to keep strong
And singing the songs but then you're gone.

I miss the way you always comfort me,
I'm sorry I could never do the same.
The path you set me on had bumps and turns
But it will be better if you just have faith.

I miss the sound of your sweet voice
Through dark times just to hear that noise
You told me what had right and wrong
But ring in my ears for far too long.

You were such a caring person
That helped and hurt me with your powerful words.
You'd guide me and mislead me through the day
You left me lonely when I'd rather you stay.

Fane Cook (13)
Northfield School & Sports College, Billingham

I'M WAITING

I'm waiting for the birds to sing,
In my lifeless bed.
I'm waiting for that one voice
Get up and sleep when you're dead.

I'm waiting for that one person
To shout my name with no shame.
I'm waiting to be freed from his hellhole
I only have myself to blame.

I'm waiting for that final moment,
When this all ends.
I'm waiting to go out in the world
When that is all depends.

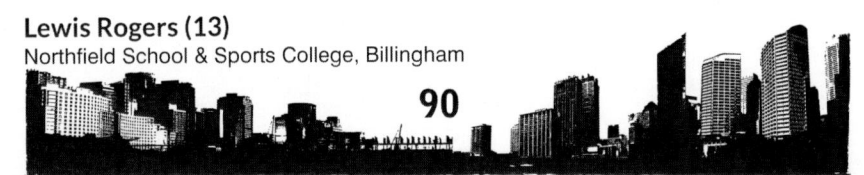

Lewis Rogers (13)
Northfield School & Sports College, Billingham

LONELINESS

I sit and stare into the night,
When I look around there's no one in sight,
Even the stars seem happy, shining in the sky,
As tears emerge from my eyes.

The concrete path, so rigid and rough,
No bed, no pillows, I guess it's tough,
That aching pain which never goes away,
But after all that's the price I have to pay.

I have nobody to look after me,
I'm all alone, you see,
Flowers, birds, tree, they don't look the same,
When there's no one to cherish them with, it's such a shame.

I have no home, only the roads,
Street after street, there's loads and loads,
All I want is somebody to love,
But I guess for now, I've only got the stars above.

Zoe Beamson (13)
Northfield School & Sports College, Billingham

LONELINESS

Life is short and life is sweet,
Never to touch but sometimes we keep;
The memories shared with ones we pass,
Life gone by, taken to fast.
You stay with me in my prayers
And I will always remember you in your golden days.

Days pass by and I am lonely without you,
But in my dreams I see you there.
So when I remember that you are here no more
I sleep and dream that in the clouds you soar.

I hear your words and you say to me,
'My darling Cloe, here I will always be.'

Cloe Laughton (13)
Northfield School & Sports College, Billingham

LONELY

My heart beats a lonely song
And I see a road, that stretches too long.
A small building lies alone
And I rest inside, my weary old bones.

I have no one else left to love
As they have all moved up, up high above.
My life is not going to go on forever,
It could end quite quick with the flick of a lever.

All I now do is work so hard
Even with my money, my opportunities are barred.
I close my eyes realising my doom,
And dare not dream that this is my tomb.

Nobody else is at my side
As I come to the end of this long and lonely ride.
Though my life was poorly lived and I fell to a dark descent,
I am still grateful though, that greatness is not carved in dry cement.

William Sherry (13)
Northfield School & Sports College, Billingham

THIS IS LONELINESS

Being alone,
Going crazy,
Nobody cares,
Nobody understands.

Independence is key,
Depression thriving within me,
Me, myself and I,
I'm the director of my own destiny.

Sitting here,
Nobody else matters,
I'm lonely,
This is loneliness.

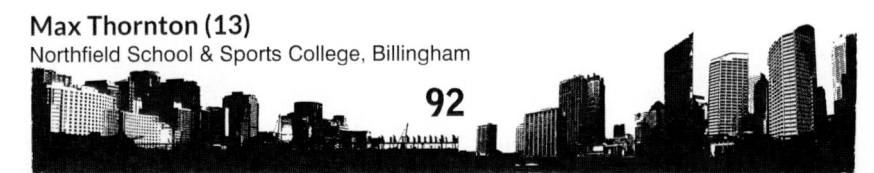

Max Thornton (13)
Northfield School & Sports College, Billingham

LONELINESS

Loneliness isn't about being on your own,
It's about having no one at the end of the phone,
It's about having no friends or family,
Being a single leaf on a tree.
During the Christmas festive season,
People can't visit, they make up a reason,
A week later when we countdown from ten,
I hear the cheers and laughter of more popular men,
They are having their party next door,
While my night is simply a bore.
It's about receiving heartbreaking bad news
And having no one to talk to, so hitting the booze.

This is my life, trapped but free,
A bright future I do not see,
No one else, only me.

Alex Jones (13)
Northfield School & Sports College, Billingham

BLANK

Everything starts as a blank canvas
Unknown, needing to find its way
Hope is all that it needs
To find something to lead its imagination.

Not knowing where to begin
A blank page, a fresh start
Desperate to create a masterpiece
But can only achieve with a guiding hand.

The stroke of a paintbrush
Gives the canvas a starting point,
A direction
Adding colour to its potential
Showing what it truly can be.

Olivia Lambert (13)
Northfield School & Sports College, Billingham

RUN AWAY

Please don't leave me by myself again,
Because without you it leaves a hole in my heart
And you left me there all on my own
With nobody to turn to for help.
My life broke down in pieces
And when I knew you weren't there
It made everything worse
It was like I wasn't the same person
Everyone I knew just disappeared
I was invisible
I couldn't hold on to what I had
And what I didn't love anymore
I didn't have you there
You didn't have me there
So I just ran away.

Amy Grey (14)
Northfield School & Sports College, Billingham

WHY?

I ran alone, wondering why,
Why no one was there
To pass me by?

I walked alone, wondering why,
Why I had no one
To kiss me goodbye?

I sat alone, wondering why,
Why the sky was dark
Why I wanted to cry?

I lay alone, wondering why,
Why everything was still
As I gave one last sigh.

Erin Wood (13)
Northfield School & Sports College, Billingham

THE MAN WITH NO FAMILY

A man walked into a room
No company but his sweeping broom
He liked to wonder as the days went by
If he had a family, but he doesn't, why?
He wonders if they'd celebrate birthdays
Or accompany him while he prays
To take him to the park
With his grandchildren in the dark.
They could bring him his Sunday lunch
And tell him stories as they munch
But no,
A man walked into a room
No company but his broom.

Alex Elizabeth Georgiou (13)
Northfield School & Sports College, Billingham

LONELINESS

A dark room filled only with the light of a single candle,
The room unseen by any creature
was a solitary shadow in the building,
The building on its own in a desolate wasteland
of shadows from the dull moon,
The area stricken of sunlight
where there is only a single object at one time always.
A single world surrounds the wasteland
in the galaxy of forgotten space.
Infinite area only one place.
The dark room holds no people
just a single candle.

Lewis Clark (14)
Northfield School & Sports College, Billingham

LOST SOUL

Who can hear me when I call?
Can anyone see me, anyone at all?
Am I here? Do I exist
Or am I a soul lost within the mist?
My body lies here in the darkness
Nothing is clear, just complete blackness.
Can you see me when I stand next to you?
Do you feel my presence in everything you do?
Why don't you see me? I don't understand.
It's like I've been deserted on my own land.
I feel so lonely, my tears start to fall
As I realise I'm not here, I am just a lost soul.

Joanna Brackstone (13)
Northfield School & Sports College, Billingham

NEVER ALONE TOO LONG

Starry-eyed, like being trapped in a cage,
Feeling anxious, nervous, becoming full of rage.

Wanting to speak, but have no words to say,
Lots of feelings that you just can't display.

You don't have to be on your own to feel lonely and sad,
You can be amongst friends or family and still feel bad.

The trick is to smile and be proud of yourself,
Keep your head held high, get down from the shelf.

Remember you are loved by family and friends,
You are special and beautiful and you break all the trends!

Regan Hoggarth (13)
Northfield School & Sports College, Billingham

SLIPPING AWAY

Darkness surrounds the room,
drips from the roof splashed onto the tiles,
nothing to listen to but the slow sound of dripping,
time slipping,
just slipping away,
nothing but time on my hands,
lonely,
it's lonely here,
it's painfully slow,
it's loud in my head but outside there's nothing.
It's lonely.

Marlee Taylor (13)
Northfield School & Sports College, Billingham

LONELY

Lonely days turn into nights,
The wind whistles out of sight.
Leaves are crunching upon the ground,
Softly and gently, not very loud.
The gorgeous smell of a moonlit bonfire,
Wrapped up warm, beginning to tire.
Hot chocolate is the start of a silent night
It's oh so lonely until morning light.

Natalie Grace Housam (13)
Northfield School & Sports College, Billingham

HOW THE WORLD HATES US

Plantation, growing upon the land,
the many scars and sores I bear on my hands.
All from the terror of the world we stand on,
we live in the life of Armageddon.
The war of humans has brought death too near,
we shall be trapped here as long as we fear.
The blackness, darkness, it's all too much,
we tremble in the sight of death as such.
This all feels quite illicit,
I feel as though I've been struck in the heart, by a pivot.
I see the face of a skull looking upon me,
looks like this is life now, for me.

Kieran Vidler (14)
Notre Dame High School, Sheffield

THE FIGHT OF MY LIFE

The arena is full of blood
The contestants have gone wild
I think I am good
I hunt in the wild.

The crowd is going crazy
The arrow is in flight
I will not be lazy
I am in a crazy fight.

I feel the wind through my fingers
I kill my enemies
I've never seen a tiger
We love our families.

I like hunting
I don't lie
My life is plummeting
I don't want to die..

Jake Hemming (12)
Penrice Academy, St Austell

THE HUNGER GAMES

T hreatening terrors getting the better of me
H orrific thoughts go around and around my aching head
E xpensive food I'm foolishly taking.

H unger Games is about to start
U rge of giving up is near, I don't know if I can go on anymore
N asty people all around wanting to make my ins my outs
G ory is definitely not the word, I don't know another that can possibly describe
E ntire arena is going against me, what am I going to do?
R ise the bow and off I go.

G ross, the smell of bodies are destroying my senses
A mazing skills I have learnt
M essing with my head is all the games are doing
E ndless confusion of why I took Prim's place
S tuck here with nowhere to run. What should I do?

Megan Paige Stone (12)
Penrice Academy, St Austell

UNTITLED

I am terrified, creeping slowly in the woods
Holding my bow and arrow and shaking in fright
Emotions going around my head
I see a dead person on the floor
I am so depressed
I walk on and see a rabbit
Dead and wet
Well that's my dinner all set.
I imagine my mum and sister at home
Sitting with no food
Starving for the rest of their lives
I wish I was there
Cooking food for them with a knife.

Jasmine Taylor (12)
Penrice Academy, St Austell

THE HUNGER GAMES

T hreatening adventures
H orrified contestants
E ndless torture

H unger Games
U tterly horrific
N othing to do, everyone dead
G uts and blood everywhere
E motions high
R evenge is on me

G lory games
A ll but one remain
M ockingjay is calling
E vil is in everyone
S ilence brews

Savannah Sanchez (12)
Penrice Academy, St Austell

THE HUNGER GAMES

T hreatening time
H orrifying emotions
E vil people begin the event

H ard to get through
U seless event that nobody wants to be in
N othing good
G ory stuff
E motional event
R idiculous riot

G enerally upsetting for the children's parents
A bsurd things
M ean mania
E choing around the world
S tupidity starts.

Tyler Kostov (12)
Penrice Academy, St Austell

THE HUNGER GAMES

T houghts of me dead
H orrified
E veryone is watching me

H unting in the wild
U nder pressure
N ever-ending
G ory games
E vil from the capital
R evenge

G oing to die
A musing for people
M essages for all
E dging towards war
S tarting to get less scared.

Katie Saunders (12)
Penrice Academy, St Austell

THE HUNGER GAMES

T hreatening adventures up ahead
H orrifying emotions ride through my head
E veryone is watching me

H ungry for children
U tterly horrified
N erve-wracking nightmares
G ory games about to start
E ndless torture
R otting away the time is ticking

G oing back in time
A fter I was ten
M um is crying
E veryone is aggravated
S ilence as I die.

Aimee Minear (12)
Penrice Academy, St Austell

THE HUNGER GAMES

T ensions high
H orrific adventure
E verlasting death

H ope for freedom
U nder pressure
N on-stop tears
G ory death
E ndless torture
R iots everywhere

G lory games
A ll but one
M ockingjay whistling
E ndless emotions
S top the games.

Blake Barnes (12)
Penrice Academy, St Austell

THE HUNGER GAMES

T ormenting terror inside of me
H orrified emotions
E xciting to be alone

H amitch will be nice
U nder relentless pressure
N ever-ending
G ory games
E ver-ending dreams
R esting at times

G oing to die
A musing for people
M essage for all
E dging to war
S tarting to enjoy it . . .

Rebekah Rowe (12)
Penrice Academy, St Austell

THE HUNGER GAMES

T hreatening adventure
H orrified emotions
E veryone is watching you

H orrified dreams
U nder the stars you die
N ever live in the Hunger Games
G etting killed
E veryone is your enemy
R eady to get killed

G od will never forgive
A nything done in a second
M ore people die than live
E veryone scared, more than scared
S oft, sweet sounds of death.

Vicky Fosten (12)
Penrice Academy, St Austell

THE HUNGER GAMES

T ormenting terror overtakes me
H eart stopping stories
E stranged people

H amitch is the coach
U nhappy people
N obody wants me
G ory deaths
E ndangering lives
R unaway

G uts spitting games
A map of death
M ental madness
E nding lives
S acrificing friends.

Joe Maunder (12)
Penrice Academy, St Austell

UNTITLED

The arena is full of blood
The crowd is going wild
I feel my heart going thud
Wild child.

The bow and arrow is in my hand
I can hear the wind blowing viciously
The horror is running through my brain

I catch a glimpse of a bird
Gliding through the arena
Everybody is watching me

Pull the bow and arrow and shoot.

Shannon Burne (12)
Penrice Academy, St Austell

UNTITLED

The crowd is going wild
The arena is full of blood
The people's names are filed
People's bodies are going to thud
We are out here all alone
People are so hungry
They have no food
Everyone is fighting to the rot of the bone
We are still wondering who is number one
We have no interest, we are still catching a fly
Seconds until the Hunger Games
Minutes until I die.

Joran Rogers (12)
Penrice Academy, St Austell

UNTITLED

Threatening terror is getting the better of me
Horrified thoughts are going around my head
Exhaustion is running through my blood
I see people falling and screaming, practising for the games
I hear people crying on and on and on through the skin of their lungs
I feel people are going to forget us if we die
I imagine people leaving, my past is just a sad blur.

Jess Harvey (12)
Penrice Academy, St Austell

GRANDPAPA SEWELL

Grandpapa Sewell is a silly old fool
He sounds very croaky when he sings karaoke
He drinks and he drinks 'til his nose is all pink
He is a silly old fool.

Grandpapa Sewell is a silly old fool
He likes the race horses and has favourite courses
He went on the soil and met Princess Royal
He likes the race horses.

Grandpapa Sewell is a silly old fool
He likes to play cricket and hits all the wickets
He umpires the team and likes clotted cream
He's a sporty Grandpapa.

Grandpapa Sewell is a silly old fool
He loves his two girlies although they're whirly
They're as daft as a brush and always in a rush
He loves his girlies.

Grandpapa Sewell is a silly old fool
He sounds very croaky when he sings karaoke
He drinks and he drinks 'til his nose is all pink
He is a silly old fool.

Penny Cleevely (11)
Pittville School, Cheltenham

MY PAIN IS A SECRET

My pain is a secret,
No one can know.
Everything you say,
I can't let it go.

You judge me all the time
And the colour of my skin.
You always call me fat,
Am I supposed to be thin?

I can't help who I am,
This is me.
I don't get up every morning
And decide who I want to be!

You don't understand,
None of you do.
You never will
Until it happens to you.

My emotions are strong,
I can't let them out.
Because of you, my mind
Is full of self-doubt.

I know I'm not perfect
None of us are
The road to happiness
Seems very far.

Please stop hurting me,
Please leave me alone,
Stop sending hurtful messages
To my iPhone.

Accept me as I am
Not how I look.
You shouldn't judge
the cover of my book.

The cuts on my leg
They hurt too,
All because of the things
You say and do.

Paris Mary Duffus (12)
Pittville School, Cheltenham

WE KILL FOR

We stand on the edge of tomorrow
But we kill tigers and hippos.
We can't get to tomorrow, not even touch it
As we still wear hunter's kit.

We kill for decoration and fun,
We hunt them down as they run.
Is an animal's life worth less than a woman's figure?
All we do is point a gun and pull the trigger.

People have pets named Tibbers or Jeff,
But they don't know about the destruction and death.
They wouldn't, people kill them.
We kill all animals, the world's gem.

No one likes to think about being pursued,
To die, to be eaten, just for food.
But for animals; it's their life,
We eat them with a fork and knife.

What do we really kill for?
Life and death, do we really decide what death is for.

Luke Smith (12)
Pittville School, Cheltenham

THE ANGER OF BULLYING

Your fist is full of so much hate,
so much it could shatter a plate.
You think it is alright to fight,
don't you know they cry at night?

You may say they're lame,
but really you're the same.
Into their chest, your foot makes a crash,
at the end of the night they just saw the white light.

You look down at the sight,
watching as they see the bright light.
Just because you are lost,
you force them to pay the cost.

You may be wearing 'armour'
but you know what will bite you . . .
Karma.

Jessica Anne Yasmin Burnham (12)
Pittville School, Cheltenham

DANCING IN THE MOONLIGHT

As the moon shines bright,
In the darkness of the night,
The movement in the trees,
The swirling of the seas.

I turn and leap through the blackness of the night,
Only the stars watching me, so dim yet so bright,
The power that I hold is strong and free,
The wildness within me is meant for the sea.

The sand beneath me is damp and fine,
I inhale its softness as I start to climb,
The whistle of the air is calm and soothing,
As I soar from the sea, rapidly moving.

My movement is fierce, vicious and tumbling,
Like an avalanche of snow rolling and crumbling,
The white of my wave, thrilling and crashing,
Towards the beach violently thrashing.

My journey has ended as I wash to the shore,
My body is empty but I wish for more,
To swirl up again in the silent night sky,
However all I do is ebb and die.

Evie Thursfield (11)
Plantsbrook School, Sutton Coldfield

INTO THE LIGHT

Look into the light
To see what you desire.
A spell it won't cast
Nor will it be a liar.

I know the light is bright
But fight through it with your fire.
Be careful, you must be fast
'Cause peace is in your grasp.

Jennifer Coull (13)
Queen Anne High School, Dunfermline

EMOTIONS

Excitement,
I can't tell you if it's the world holding their breath or if it's me
And I can't tell if it's the earth that's shaking or if it's my heart.
It feels like an earthquake has erupted beneath my feet
And somewhere deep within me, I'm so terribly excited.

It feels like someone caught a zoo of butterflies and caged them in my stomach.
I feel bubbly from head to toe,
My blood is boiling with excitement,
My heart is warming me up,
I'm excited.

Happiness,
We waste most of our time looking for the one thing we all desire, happiness
But what we all don't know is that happiness lies in everything,
Even the littlest things.

Happiness lies in a summer's day, where the sun is up
And the sky is in a shade of blue,
Happiness lies in people we love, a lover, a friend, a family member.
Happiness lies in a good cup of tea and a friend we share good conversations with.
Happiness lies in wonderful moments, it lies in music,
The ones we dance and sing to.
Happiness hides in someone's laughter
And a smile so bright, it lights up everyone's heart.
I am happy.

Fear,
Screams in the pitch-black, turns butterflies to moths,
Delicate wings beating wisps of air.
Invisible people touching, reaching, grabbing, pulling
And curling around each part of the body at all times,
The feeling creeps into the mind.
Tossing on the blankets in bed, latching and grasping to them,
Hands held on so tight that the knuckles go white
And ache with a deepness, like the deepness of a black hole.

Violently flailing, scratching, clawing,
None of them will win the bottle,
It grips us in the time of our own darkness.
I'm scared.

Anger,
Black mind, cloudy vision, the satisfying collision
From an elbow swung or a punch thrown
And in my ears a buzzing drone.
I breathe deeply and start to think of how I was pushed to the brink,
I really do regret it now,
I'd fix it but I don't know how.

But it feels so good at the same time
But the mind doing it isn't mine.
It's the nice sweet child with a polite voice and good manners.

But which am I and which is me?
Which one of them am I going to be?
The child that's weak but nice or not.
I'm angry.

Lee Hynd (11)
Queen Anne High School, Dunfermline

THE HEADLIGHTS

The car carries on, not a care in the world,
A poor boy lies injured, his body curled,
I stand startled, to see this awful sight,
Shivering cold, on a dark and stormy night.

To think that he was just minutes away,
From seeing his family, one special day,
But all of that was taken away, by the blinding beams of sadness,
This horrible crash was the worst day to end the awful day of madness.

Lily Smith (12)
Queen Anne High School, Dunfermline

O MASTER OF THE TREES

Vidar's eye is summer blue,
the same colour as the moon is too.
He'll hop, he'll jump, he'll skip and fly.
To follow him I would not try.

He may seem strange, he may seem odd.
He doesn't seem to have a job.
But secretly in evergreen woods
you'll find him making very weird hoots.

He'll hoot, he'll chirp, he'll squeak and squawk
all day long as he walks.
If you were a bird you would have heard
something like this.

'Come high, come low, come quick, come slow,
come tell me what you've seen.
Tell me who has been walking through
my dark and ancient trees.'

The birds replied; some bold, some shy:

'We know who, we know who,
has been walking through the trees.
They are not much, it's just a bunch
of hungry, surly fleas.'

'Oh is that all?' said Vidar tall.
He stopped and looked at his feet.
'Oh yes, oh yes,' replied the birds,
'O master of the trees!'

Lisa Van Delft (14)
Queen Anne High School, Dunfermline

WHAT IS HOME?

What is home?
Home is a place of salvation away from war.

What is home?
Home is my motto to continue
Being the best person in me.

What is home?
Home is a heat in the Arctic
Turning your frozen fear into warm confidence.

What is home?
Home is the vault that holds all your past memories.

What is home?
Home is a pirate ship sailing across your ocean of love.

What is home?
Home is the first word you ever said.

What is home?
Home is the everlasting bond between you and your family.

What is home?
Home is the cure for fear and sadness.

Grant Waddell (11)
Queen Anne High School, Dunfermline

LAKE LOUISE

My family and I
Lake Louise.
Hear water.
Smell sunflowers.
Rocky mountains.
The lake,
Blue cloudless sky above.
Kayaks on water.
Peace and calm.

Ross Inglis (13)
Queen Anne High School, Dunfermline

THE FIRE

Crackle, crackle, crackle,
As I hear the sounds of orange and red flames,
Roar as heat blasts from the fireplace.
We sit in a semi-circle with marshmallows on skewers.
They turn brown and melt inside,
Some of them catch fire!
As we sit around the blazing flames,
A guitar starts to play.
'You light the spark in my bonfire heart,'
We sing at the top of our lungs.
The liveliness hits us all,
We are enlightened by the spirit that brings us together as one.
As we all start to drift off,
The strings stop strumming and we all stop singing.
The fire is the only light left in the darkness of the night.
As we lay our heads on our soft hands,
A lullaby plays in our heads,
''Cause our love keeps us safe through the dark night skies,
Can you sing me a last lullaby?'
Silence . . .

Jack Douglas (13)
Queen Anne High School, Dunfermline

CHRISTMAS!

C andles smelling of warm cinnamon.
H o! Ho! Ho! Santa has arrived,
R udolph is leading the way.
I t's Jesus' birthday!
S o many excited children pretending to sleep.
T he decorations gleam in the moonlight.
M orning, it's Christmas!
A terribly excited child races downstairs to rip open their presents,
S anta's job is done for the year.

Maisie Pirrie (12)
Queen Anne High School, Dunfermline

THE HORSE

Running free,
Mane swaying,
Hooves clicking,
Bucking and neighing.

Silky coat,
Strong tail,
Twitchy ears,
Coarse and pale.

Singing his song to the rhythm of the breeze,
What a smart creature,
He gallops with ease.

I can see his breath
In the cold night air,
He's probably searching for his foal and mare.

His strong voice,
Rough and hoarse,
This is why I love my horse.

Jody Wright (12)
Queen Anne High School, Dunfermline

LIGHT

When there is no light I curl up tight
And go to sleep in bed,
When the light shines bright
I get up and sigh, as the blue birds flutter by.

The orange-yellow beams of sun
Blind me as I walk,
But soon it goes and I walk home
To meet my friends and talk.

India McKendry (11)
Queen Anne High School, Dunfermline

THE SUN

Far, far away,
Miles past the moon,
There is one special star
Like a giant yellow balloon.

How is it so hot?
How is it so bright?
As we spin around it,
All day and night.

There are so many questions!
Maybe there is other life,
Like aliens and monsters
Carrying spears and knives.

It is a very special star,
There is only one
And it is called the sun.

Scarlett Dunn (11)
Queen Anne High School, Dunfermline

A PEACEFUL DREAM

P eace to me is not what you'd imagine it to be
E ach and everyone of us would respect everyone's human rights
A nyone and everyone should not be judged on things that they believe
C an we please just remember that we are all equal members of this wonderful world
E nd all this cruelty and stop separating everyone into groups and always remember 'love thy neighbour'. Bring peace to the world.

Molly Kelman (14)
Queen Anne High School, Dunfermline

A NEW DAY

As the shining sun stared at me in the sky,
I felt the morning breeze come rushing by.

I opened my eyes to a brand new day,
Hoping today will be the day the sun will stay.

Outside with my friends, what fun we will have;
Enjoying the sun and having a laugh.

Dark clouds stay away, we want the glimmering sun,
Having a magnificent time and fabulous fun.

As the sun begins falling, getting lower in the sky,
Sunset approaches with birds flying by.

The day's nearly over as the darkness sets in,
But tomorrow's a new day, oh where to begin?

Caitlin Malcolm (12)
Queen Anne High School, Dunfermline

AS THE LIGHT FLOWS IN

As the light flows in
My heart will flow out.
As it slowly leaves my soul you shall stay in my body.
Even though my heart is out at sea you shall stay in with me.
Even though the water is deep I can see my heart glisten
Deep, deep under the sea.

That is when I know my light is gone.

Brooke Gardner (12)
Queen Anne High School, Dunfermline

FIREWORKS

As the darkness flows
There's a loud *bang!*
And colours shoot up from the surface
Illuminating the cold dark sky
Lots of magnificent colours and shapes
As the fireworks fade they are still lurking in the sky.
Light.

Abbie Susan Gorman (12)
Queen Anne High School, Dunfermline

THE HOPE OF LIGHT

Light, light, it's a wonderful thing,
It brings us hope in our darkest hours,
But still there it is dancing in front of our eyes.
Never extinguished, always there to help us on our roller coaster lives,
Up and down we go through the times we hate and love,
But then again the light is there helping us through our lives.

Megan White (11)
Queen Anne High School, Dunfermline

THE CHICKEN

She waddles like a duck
But she's not.
She has a beak like a pigeon
But she's not.
She has fluffy hands like a human
But she's not.
She's Iris the chicken.

Charlotte Alice, Kathleen Charleston (12)
Queen Anne High School, Dunfermline

THE TRENCHES

Bullets blocking out the dull grey sky
Shell shock is killing me day by day
I can hardly stand
No food, I think the lads have started eating the rats
I would kill for a good meal and a lie down
Literally.

Andrew Savage (12)
Queen Anne High School, Dunfermline

SPORTS

S killed players
P ersistence all the way
O vercome your fears
R ise up to the top and maintain your place
T ry new things, you never know what you're good at until you try it
S truggling is not in my vocabulary.

Kallum S Gallacher (11)
Queen Anne High School, Dunfermline

WINTER

Ice-cold touch from the winter god.
The ice from the floor melts into glistening water.
Your colour fades from the icy wind.
You slide on the ice but keep falling in your mind.
You throw snowballs to have some fun
But you're hurting the person.

Alistair Patten (12)
Queen Anne High School, Dunfermline

FIREWORKS

I see a light in the sky,
There are lots of different colours
And shapes that light up the night.
They make lots of noise,
Then disappear into the night!
Bang!

Keela Rutherford (12)
Queen Anne High School, Dunfermline

DUBAI

D ubai is an awesome place
U nder the scalding sun
B iggest skyscraper
A really big shopping centre
I feel different emotions.

Calum Dalton (11)
Queen Anne High School, Dunfermline

STREETLIGHT

Wow, it's bright
All day, all night
The streetlights light up the sky
They make me feel safe, but why?

Luke Fleming (11)
Queen Anne High School, Dunfermline

FIREWORKS

The fireworks explode in different colours
Lighting up the sky.
When they burst they look like flowers
Or bullets zooming at the speed of light.

Tyrone Farlam (12)
Queen Anne High School, Dunfermline

LIGHT

In December I look out at night
And I see all the Christmas tree lights.
I see red, I see green
And that makes me feel excited for the days to come.

Calum Law (12)
Queen Anne High School, Dunfermline

LIGHT

Twinkling tree lights
Fireflies fluttering by
Stars shining in the silver moonlight
I feel warm and comforted by these dazzling lights.

Erin Edwards (12)
Queen Anne High School, Dunfermline

I AM A HURRICANE!

For some reason I can't explain
I am feeling a deluge of emotions.
I am angry, and sad and I am about to break out
I can't stand this anymore!
As I rise and shout
All you can hear is thunder booming, loud.

Flying debris is in the air
And floods are everywhere.
I cry but it comes out as cold, driving rain which I can't see through.
People are swept away crying for their loved ones
Shouting and screaming, 'Help! Help!'

I am ashamed of what I've done
I've destroyed towns and people's lives.
My violent blowing winds stop abruptly
So do my tears, but then, they start up again.

As my temper subsides, I start to feel remorse.
Lightning is flashing just like the flashbacks in my head.
I am annoyed with myself, with what I've done.
I am dying now, hurricanes can only strike once
As I walk to the horizon the people left celebrate that I am gone.

Sofia Deplidge
Rossall School, Fleetwood

THE WOLF

I feel sorry for the wolf.
Its sheer size scaring people!

Its magnificent paws planting prints in the snow . . .
The wolf's fur, gleaming with white blossom, like magnolia.
Dancing better than any ballerina I've seen.

The cubs frolic around
Whilst their mother watches vigilantly over them.
She knows that one day
They will be doing likewise.

One springtime morn,
The trio tentatively trotted through the wood . . .
Then 'she' heard gunfire
And a deer fell to the ground,
Only twenty metres away from her beloved pack.

They ran
Through the trees!
Through the stream!
They were the spirit of the wind!
With valiant effort
They nevertheless come face to face with the 'hunter.'

The mother bared her teeth.
The hunter backed off!

I feel sorry for the wolf.
Its sheer size scaring people!

Jude Blakeley (13)
Royds Hall Community School, Huddersfield

BEING BRITISH

(Lipogram – A)

Being British is like belonging to the 'Exclusive Club'
With lists of conduct which you must follow
Extensive number of rules must be obeyed
To give one's stiff upper lip

Some of the requirements of being British include;
Continuous hot drink consumption
From one's expensive crockery
Complete with one's biscuit of choice

The funny thing with us Brits
Is our obsession with forming rows
From the doctors to the Post Office
Queuing is *the* constitutive tool of being British

Some imply our humour is dry
Most often our friends from over the pond
It is quoted from time to time,
London gin is more quenching!

Mr Bond is his title
007 is his number
Exquisite vehicles become his currency
Technology is his sword

Queenie sits upon her throne
Protecting the Empire
Her subjects bow before her divine power
But Will's wife, wields the key to British minds

But now it is time for my poem to end
This piece discusses some of our quirks
But it brings just sips
From the cup which is being British.

Morgan Willetts (14)
St Joseph's College, Ipswich

MRS PRATCHETT

Mrs Pratchett,
Mrs Pratchett
Oh so mean
And never ever clean.

Mrs Pratchett,
Mrs Pratchett
Oh so thin,
I wonder if she can fit in a bin.

Mrs Pratchett,
Mrs Pratchett
Oh so dirty,
I wonder if she does her own laundry.

Mrs Pratchett,
Mrs Pratchett
Oh so vicious,
I wonder if she can make anything delicious.

Mrs Pratchett,
Mrs Pratchett
Oh so bitter,
I wonder if she has ever thought of being sweeter.

Mrs Pratchett,
Mrs Pratchett
Oh so horrible,
She never finds anything adorable.

Mrs Pratchett,
Mrs Pratchett
Her hands are always black,
It's like she has had a black attack,
You won't stand a chance.

Madeleine Cooke (11)
St Joseph's College, Ipswich

MY DOG HAS FLEAS

My dog has fleas
Scratch, scratch, scratch.
Always on the move,
Scratch, scratch, scratch.
Can't keep still,
Scratch, scratch, scratch.
The dog,
Scratch, scratch, scratch.

My dad is mad,
Scratch, scratch, scratch.
'Get that dog out!'
Scratch, scratch, scratch.
'No,' yells Mum.
Scratch, scratch, scratch.
'It's not her fault.'
Scratch, scratch, scratch.

'Run a bath,' I yell.
Scratch, scratch, scratch.
The dog has gone mad.
Scratch, scratch, scratch.
Get some flea shampoo.
Scratch, scratch, scratch.

Put the shampoo on,
Scratch, scratch, scratch.
Massage well.
Mmmmmmmmmm,
Lovely.
Mmmmmmmmmm,
More lovely.
The dog is dry, all is quiet.

Helena Chan (11)
St Joseph's College, Ipswich

THE DREAM

We devote our lives to it,
It takes determination and grit,
We get better bit by bit,
The more time we give to it.

We won't quit, if our lives depend on it,
The joy we get out of it, from that one big hit.

We sacrifice everything,
For our team,
To be the champions,
Is our single dream.

We push our bodies, to the absolute extreme,
To get the most movement, off that seam.

Now is the time
For us to excel,
Forget about past mistakes,
No need to dwell.

It is the thing that you decide to play,
Enjoying with friends, each and every day.

Our ambition is to be,
The first one to score,
I'll be the one,
To receive that roar
That winning pass will be mine,
The guy on the other end, taps it past the goal line.

Wherever you play,
Maybe number eight,
When the game begins,
It's up to you to decide your fate.

Matthew Kent (13)
St Joseph's College, Ipswich

MY PARALLEL UNIVERSE

In my parallel universe
I dream of a place where all is well
With our minds, bodies and souls
Everything that's natural and good
Being treated well and never misunderstood

Boys and girls filled with laughter
Rejoicing along the open streets, being well looked after
Not having a single care in the world
Being completely free, and staying unconcerned
But so far, only this can I dream

I also once dreamed of a place united
Where black and white together could be sighted
Not being judged at one's first glance
But instead, together could just dance
Yet again, only this can I dream

I dream that there will be no war, just peace
And that the persecuted
Will be able to settle down with ease
People making a positive contribution
With absolutely no nuclear fusion

I can see the light at the end of the tunnel
And know that one day we will reach it
Even if there is a slight fumble

We are slowly getting there, day by day
So I'll continue to dream once more
Of when we'll walk through the open door
And enter into, my parallel universe
Which will hopefully be shared and loved by us all.

Isaac Codjoe (13)
St Joseph's College, Ipswich

ABUSE/ANXIETY

I walk... I run...
It's something I'll never overcome...

You know those fears inside your head?
Trembling terror is all they spread.
You know those voices screaming?
Mine are my everlasting demons.
Isolation and fear have trapped me
Like a blind child; I cannot see.
I deserve more, we all do,
So why, I ask does no one pull through?
Someone to break down these walls, guarded by my past
Someone to run to my side, now, fast

After all this time the clocks have changed,
I finally broke free from my rusty chains.
You were my demons and you were my walls,
Abuse is the beast I tamed and called.
You were the puppet master, I was your doll,
Stuck in a clear box with no control.
You acted like a bull in a china store,
I'm the vase you smashed on the floor.
But like a phoenix I rose up
And from here on out things can only go up.

I walk... I run...
It's something I've finally overcome.

Sophie Wykes (14)
St Joseph's College, Ipswich

WHAT IS INSPIRATION?

(Lipogram – E)

For such oddity of inspiration,
How can you assign a tag?
Fully constant and durably dynamic,
How charmingly it lights
That crucial spark in your soul
Which says this is it,
This is what I work for!

Doth grant armour
Fit for disrupting worlds
Fit for shifting mountains
'Tis crucial as cool bracing air
Furnishing our lungs.
It abducts, nay, hooks its victim
Swaying thoughts, luring charisma.

Though still as a gift
Fraught with flair,
Author of raw truths,
Initiator of fruitful product,
A champion of doubt
Pushing you on and on
Until nothing is abiding in you
But a murmur forcing you to hang on.

Louise Humphries
St Joseph's College, Ipswich

BESIDE THE WATER

(Lipogram – O)

As I dance beside the water
All my senses laugh and sing,
The white waves crashing as he taught her,
Salty fingers brush the bird's wing.

As I stand beside the water,
I recall the brilliant tales it tells,
What shining shells and pebbles it gave her,
Salty fingers drag them under
And facing the beach, they bid farewell.

As I sit beside the water,
I can relax and listen intently,
As the glasses held by desperate children caught her,
Salty fingers entice me gently.

As I lay beside the water,
My features dampen and I can't hear
And I think *can I accept her?*
Salty fingers get near and near.

As I slip beneath the water,
Everything I see is black,
The sea has finally dragged me under,
Salty fingers never setting me back . . .

Isabelle Atkinson (12)
St Joseph's College, Ipswich

HALLOWEEN

(Lipogram – U)

Cobwebs on the windows,
Skeletons on the door we're decorating for Halloween once more.
Zombie, vampire, Frankenstein, so many to choose from,
Which freak will I be this year?
Blood dripping from my lips, scars painted on my face,
Deathly white skin, it's face paint time again.
Mini rolls oozing with green icing,
Marshmallow ghosts on top of orange cakes,
Black spiders make the party food complete.
Silly string ready, preparing to frighten visitors
Who dare to knock for sweets.
Giggling, shoving, playing, we're excited in anticipation
Of the treats we might find.
Something scrapes against my hair, I spin . . .
Phew, nothing is there.
A howl and a cackle, we glance at each other
And make a dash for it,
Desperate to escape the witches and werewolves.
The door slams, we collapse into fits of giggles,
And reality is different now we are safe inside the home.
Lying in bed there's a terrible groan,
It's my stomach crammed with too many sweets.

Isabella Grylls (12)
St Joseph's College, Ipswich

MY FEATHER FRIENDS

I have a little friend, Red Chest, who sits upon my wall,
I feed him from my plate before I go to school.

I have a magnificent garden with magnificent feather friends,
Great tits in the undergrowth and a sweet little wren.

Then of course a woodpecker and not forgetting a jay,
Oh I love my garden with my lovely feather friends.

Archie Mariani (11)
St Joseph's College, Ipswich

SAD LOVE

(Lipogram – A)

I miss you more
I thought I would
I cried much more
I did not think

Time sorts most
It's this they shout
But love's the price
So I give up

Sometimes I smile
I know you're close
It's not enough
You're not here

Time rolls by
It's not like it used to be
Yet deep down
You still belong

You left love behind
When you flew
But my piece of you
Is not enough.

William Marston (12)
St Joseph's College, Ipswich

THE POOR OLD LADY

(Lipogram – I)

A lady she sat on the bus
And started to make a huge fuss.
Cos on the next seat
Was an ape with large feet.
'Move over, there's no room for us!'

Harry Smith (11)
St Joseph's College, Ipswich

MRS PRATCHET

Mrs Pratchet
Is a little hatchet.
She's cruel with all her heart
And she's good at that part.
She's got long cheesy nails
As long as a rat's tail.
She always has a terrible grin
When it comes to children.
When you step closer and closer
Your heart stops beating.
She's bitter and she's as tasteless as a pitta bread.
When you eat your favourite sweets from the jar
She leaves traces of oily fingerprints.
Beware Mrs Pratchet
That little hatchet.
She's as skinny as your hand,
She's as tight as a band.
Her face is as cruel as ever,
She's wicked in her own ways.
The moment you see her
Your heart beats way into the distance.
You could just hear her from miles away.

Grace Ali (11)
St Joseph's College, Ipswich

THE LION

Deafening is the lion's roar.
Heard as far as land could go,
Something I'd only imagined before,
But after that experience, I would know
Deafening is the lion's roar.

True beauty is the lion's mane.
A big cat with a head of flames,
A beast like him feels no pain,
An osset that gives a lion its name,
True beauty is the lion's mane.

Real elegance is the lion's stature,
Filled with pride, standing strong.
A lion's motif is to capture
Looking good all day long,
Real elegance is the lion's stature.

Helpless is the lion's prey.
'What's for dinner?' Take your pick!
He settles down and munches away,
While his friends ask, 'What's your trick?'
Helpless is the lion's prey.

Taylor Locke (13)
St Joseph's College, Ipswich

DARCY

Darcy, Darcy, she is very flighty,
She keeps us up by being Darcy.
Darcy, Darcy, she is very dancy,
She keeps us up by being Darcy.
Darcy, Darcy, she is very bouncy,
She keeps us up by being Darcy.
Darcy, Darcy, she is very portly,
She keeps us up by being Darcy.
Darcy, Darcy, she is very itchy,
She keeps us up by being Darcy.
Darcy, Darcy, she is very barky,
She keeps us up by being Darcy.
Darcy, Darcy, she is very lovely,
She keeps us up by being Darcy.
Darcy, Darcy, she is very ugly,
She keeps us up by being Darcy.
Darcy, Darcy, she is very horsey,
She keeps us up by being Darcy.
Darcy, Darcy, she is very feisty,
She keeps us up by being Darcy.
Darcy, Darcy is simply Darcy.

Joshua Robert Anthony Palmer (11)
St Joseph's College, Ipswich

THE KEYBOARD

The keyboard black, the text an elegant shade of white.
A beautiful metropolitan style, dark covered by light.
When you type it's a joy, oh such a joy!
But with the words you may type, this is not a toy.
Racial slurs, offensive words and other terms abusive
Things only typed by those who are socially reclusive
When people type these things, they refrain from innocence,
However you cannot deny a keyboard's elegance,
Such elegance, such elegance.

The keyboard is a beautiful, intelligent tool!
It can be used by a genius or even a fool.
As is evident from my previous verse,
For an intelligent phrase, far you must traverse.
Let it be known though, for those under a bridge
There are certain rules, which you must not resist.
Some people decide to accuse people of being quite queer
Others just type 'Free phone, click here!'
When people type these things, they refrain from innocence
However you cannot deny a keyboard's elegance,
Such elegance, such elegance.

William Francisco Scoones (13)
St Joseph's College, Ipswich

THE WATER WAS BURNING

(Lipogram – D)

The water was burning, burning away,
It may not be here in a future May,
The reason for this terrible affair,
Is the avarice of man and his lack of care.

He ought to have known that water is a must,
It is the only thing to quench a thirst,
Look after your planet and remember this,
Without your help it will not exist.

Jessica Bryce (13)
St Joseph's College, Ipswich

WINTER

The weather is cold and bleak,
People huddled together by a fire,
The robins are chirping,
Their red chests glowing in the snow,
The hats and scarves come out again,
Christmas is approaching.

Families gather together now,
For this special time of year,
Presents are given and opened,
Love is spread all around,
And one time of year brings all this,
It's the cold, glowing, love sharing,
Winter.

After winter comes the spring,
Newborn lambs and flowers,
The weather gets warmer,
Winter is over,
Until another year.

Rhiannon Dunbar (13)
St Joseph's College, Ipswich

LIPOGRAM – I

(Lipogram – I)

A true test of character
A true test of courage
A true test of sportsmen
The taste of sweat
The feel of mud
The appearance of opponents
The sound of the crowd
A true test of character
A true test of courage
A true test of a sportsman.

Jack Oakes (14)
St Joseph's College, Ipswich

HAPPINESS

(Lipogram – J)

Happiness is a skill,
Life can go uphill,
It is like a roller coaster,
It can give you a thrill.

Happiness never ends,
You can share it with your friends,
They adore it too,
Your personality will extend.

Happiness is unpredictable,
People cannot be critical,
It can never end in pain,
It could end in a miracle.

Happiness is fun,
It shines like the sun,
But you can go near it,
Bye because my poem is done.

Oscar Bolton (11)
St Joseph's College, Ipswich

OCEAN

I t is as calm as a summer's breeze
N evertheless it's as serene as a hurricane
D espite just being as blaring as a band
I n spite that it's really just a whisper
A nd it is really just fascinating
N ow what can I see?

O r what it can be?
C hilly as ice
E ven though it's preferably quite nice
A nd at the end
N owadays it might just attend.

Tom Marshlain (12)
St Joseph's College, Ipswich

THE RISING EVIL

(Lipogram – A)

Evil is rising,
There's lots of signs,
You just need to look for them,
Come on, use your mind.

The twilight is upon us,
Bright futures you won't see,
Just lock up your windows,
Then be rid of the key.

Listen very closely to the sinister howls,
Then you'll know when it's coming,
When to you it is bound.

The time is upon us,
The time is right now,
But don't you go venture,
Or else you'll be found.

Elana Sophia Fraser (15)
St Joseph's College, Ipswich

WALKING ALONG THE BEACH

I walk along the beach,
The sun is glistening on the sea,
Everything is calm,
No bird in sight,
Just me,
Walking along the beach.

I walk along the beach,
The aroma of the salty water,
Wind is warm on my face,
Soft sand on my feet,
Just me,
Walking along the beach.

Alex Mann (13)
St Joseph's College, Ipswich

THE MORNING SHORES...

As the sun rises high in the sky so my journey begins
Every day, off to school not knowing which adventures I will see
Wrabness Woods and here he is, Phil The Pheasant pecking in the road, silly bird
Onwards towards the river and the morning gathering is strong today
Mistley Hill and the water is glistening like sparkling diamonds
Tiny white sail boats bobbing with happiness as the sea shouts hello
We reach The Walls at Manningtree, what a feast of birds to see
Canada Geese take flight in a row so razor-sharp in a line like red arrows
Oh there she is, Rosie Red Shank walking with her red cocktail sticks
Grumpy swans hissing in the wind
Along to the amazing White Bridge
Cameron the Cormorant stands high on his post
With his wings stretched out like a vulture ready to pounce
What a wonderful journey I have in the morning.

Reubin Campbell (12)
St Joseph's College, Ipswich

AUTUMN

The leaves floating about
People looking at the shadows of yellows
Houses becoming nice and cosy
Milky hot chocolates and chai teas
Woolly hats and mittens keeping us toasty.

Wooden logs set alight in front of the sofa
A book in hand with a blanket on my lap
The cat and dog slowly dozing off
On the comfy and fuzzy mat
Mum's knitting another blanket.

The scented candles, slowly melting away
Making the house smell of pumpkin pie.

Kirsten Parsons (13)
St Joseph's College, Ipswich

BULLYING

Here in my room standing around,
When all of a sudden I was on the ground.
Tall with dark hair stood a strong man,
Ready to pound me as hard as he can.
Reaching out ready for a swipe from his hand,
I sat there waiting, terribly mad.

I got up the very next day,
To discover that there he lay.
With worry and fear,
I said, 'Quick come here, come here.'

His head in my arms he was as sick as could be,
I kneeled there beside him very desperately.
Awaiting for news in fear,
I saw him just disappear,
Out of sight he went,
There was nothing I could do to prevent.

Katie Warne (13)
St Joseph's College, Ipswich

RUGBY TACKLE

(Lipogram – O)

The ball is in my hand, it feels hard, bumpy and wet,
My heart begins to race as I run as fast as I can,
The wind hits my face as I scan the pitch,
I zip and dart between three players,
When, *thwack!*
I feel four arms hit my legs.
It feels like time is passing by,
As I hit the freezing, hard dirt.
I hit the dirt, trying to get my team the ball,
I smell sweat and anger.
I can hear my team saying, 'Get him!'
I can taste the sweat with a metal stud in my cheek.

Dominic Terry Raines (12)
St Joseph's College, Ipswich

FIREWORKS

(Lipogram – A)

People will cluster together to see
The fireworks, looking like tiny rockets lighting the sky
The scent of gunpowder clogs the night sky, drifting round the night
Sounding like tiny bullets colliding together.

Fireworks tremble the ground under your feet
The gunpowder smell clings to your mouth, sweet but foul
Colour lights up the sky for miles, the broken sound of thunder
Lights drop slowly through the night dying, growing dimmer.

Crowds cheer, hiss with every burst, the light reflects in their eyes
Suddenly eruptions of colour rise from the ground
The crowds come up, then show their enjoyment
But slowly the show comes to its end.

The people dissolve home, out of the cold,
But the drone of fireworks still rings outside.

Harry Suckling
St Joseph's College, Ipswich

HER EYES

Her eyes were like water ways,
And he loved the way they flooded,
Like great tsunamis crashing down her cheeks.

Her eyes were like water ways,
And he loved the way they glittered,
Like stars sparkling in the night.

Her eyes were like water ways,
And he loved the way they hypnotised him,
Like a dream he could never awake from.

Her eyes were like water ways,
And he loved the way they flooded,
But in the end she drowned.

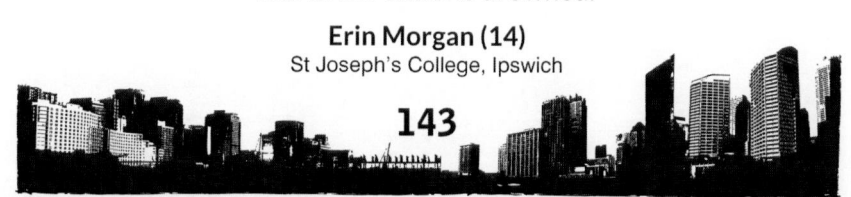

Erin Morgan (14)
St Joseph's College, Ipswich

PERFECT SUNLIGHT

You wait until darkness, you don't sleep at night,
This is how you catch perfect sunlight.

The ghosts and the ghouls come out to play,
You won't even see the light of day.

First the werewolves let out their menacing howl
Then the vampires start to growl.

The perfect sunlight is drawing near,
Hush everyone there's no reason to fear.

This is the end of the terrible dark,
You hear in the distance the hounds of Hell bark.

The perfect sunlight is at the top of the hill
So you stop there and stand still.

Everyone falls quiet, you can rest
Because this is the end of the ongoing quest.

Lily Henshall Howar (12)
St Joseph's College, Ipswich

YULE

What is the occasion? Yule!
Sneak and ascend the steps in a quiet fashion,
Open the gifts, explode with joy,
But don't let the boys make a fool out of Yule.

The lights stay on and push away the bites of light.
May the angels be singing and let the bells start beating.
Join in with the singing, you might stop tingling.

Let the holidays be flooded with thousands of gifts
And may the company of Yule be happy and pleasant.

It's Yule, so don't be a fool.

Katerina Everard (12)
St Joseph's College, Ipswich

RUGBY

I love roaring places,
Where the crowd is cheering for me,
To get to the try line,
I smell the sweet aroma of grass,
As I hit the floor my hands are anaesthetised,
I slam-slam-slam the ball into the earth,
I see the scoreboard change,
Six-nil.
I taste the feeling of accomplishment right there,
Will I ever be a saint?
Tick-tock, tick-tock!
I see ...
Zero-zero-zero-zero on the clock,
The noise is almost like snakes hissing,
Where can I get a hot bath
And relax my tired bones?

Dantay Ward (11)
St Joseph's College, Ipswich

THE RABBIT

(Lipogram – Z)

Rabbit; oh rabbit, at home with his brothers,
Playing hide-and-seek under the covers,
Munching on carrots all night long,
Don't be too greedy or you'll get a sore tum.

Rabbit; oh rabbit, running across the land,
Be careful, you don't want to end up being peeled.
You must make sure you stay close to the home
And a distance away from the agricultural worker's dome.

Rabbit; oh rabbit, all velvety ears,
Listen out, vixen's about, or it could end in tears.
Always jumping and sprinting around,
Life is exciting with adventures abound.

Cameron Towers (11)
St Joseph's College, Ipswich

THE LIGHT IN THE DARK

The faint flicker of a flame,
Coming from the window,
The rolling downpour of rain,
The clock ticking to and fro,
A howl of a dog,
A creak from a door,
Thick grey fog,
Water on the floor,
The haunted hall
Of the haunted manor,
A cry and a call,
The flickering banner,
The deep imprint of a rubber tyre,
A deafening high-pitch bark,
Within a fraction of a moment, the light expired
And everything but the flame is dark.

Leo Bignell (12)
St Joseph's College, Ipswich

DOGS

(Lipogram – E)

An animal is a cuddly thing,
You laugh and cry with it,
If your animal is sad play with it,
You know if it's purring.

An animal is a warm thing,
It's cuddly and it will bark at you back,
It has the option to lift you out of tough days,
Right from the start, it will always kiss you
And you will kiss it back.

Lucy Waring (12)
St Joseph's College, Ipswich

MY LIPOGRAM

(Lipogram – I)

Black smells the same as snuffed out candle wax
And sounds the same as the deep dark death hole
Absorbing you into a dark black hole
How do you escape from the black?
Black, overloaded with secrets
And unsolved conundrum
Black, the end
Black absorbs you all
Even you.

Edward Lucking (12)
St Joseph's College, Ipswich

THE MIDNIGHT TIGER

The midnight tiger, in the little light of night,
Went on its midnight sight,
Looking for its prey under the box
But did not realise there was a fox.
Quickly the tiger pounced but the fox hid behind,
The tiger on its midnight sight is once again strolling slowly
Until the fox under the box woke once more,
The fox pounced on the tiger,
This time the tiger fell to the ground,
This is the story of the midnight tiger's stroll.

Patrick Rawlins (12)
St Joseph's College, Ipswich

ELOISE

The tying of her laces before she goes to battle,
The ball, the boots, the bat, some wickets or even a net,
A weapon or a tool for the challenge that lays ahead,
The blowing of the whistle,
The banging of the gun,
She is ready and prepared for the game to be won,
Passes or tackles and sprints and shots,
Tension and pressure from first till last,
In goes a shot with a fantastic blast,
Victory is hers and long may it last.

Eloise Ward (11)
St Joseph's College, Ipswich

SPOOKY

Spooky nights are full of frights
Especially the night called Halloween
Ghosts and ghouls
Make some things cruel
To give you a fright.
Trick or treat,
Sweets to eat.
Pumpkins lit,
Bats *flit, flit*
All to make a haunted Halloween Night.

Bailey Scannell (11)
St Joseph's College, Ipswich

AN AUTUMN'S DAY

An autumn's day
Very warm and bright
Filling me with merry delight
The bright leaves
The bright blue skies
Always starting with a nice sunrise
The birds chirping
The wind breathing
The skies are never grey
We all like an autumn's day.

Chidera Mary-Josephine Nwenyi (13)
St Joseph's College, Ipswich

ART GALLERY

(Lipogram – U)

Paintings hanging on the wall
Portraits made to last
Half a dozen faces speak
A message from the past

Words of warning travel down,
History's darkest years,
Beware, take care, heed my advice,
This is beyond thy deepest fears.

Katy Heron (12)
St Joseph's College, Ipswich

A THOUGHTFUL BOY

Little by little I will get ready for the great opportunities for me
But to always remember that I should not always spend my time away
I have to exercise twice a day.
Little by little I shall learn all the things I need to be great.
I must not be popular to be great.
I can be great in my own way.
I have to remember that study without play
Will make me a dull, thoughtful boy.

Nmachi Judith Chidi-Lloyd (10)
St Joseph's College, Ipswich

THE MORNING SHORES

As the sun rises high in the sky so my journey begins
Every day off to school not knowing which adventures I will see
Wrabness Woods and here he is Phil the pheasant pecking in the road, silly bird
Onwards towards the river and the morning gathering is strong today
Mistley Hill and the water is glistening like sparkling diamonds
Tiny white sail boats bobbing with happiness as the sea shouts 'Hello'
We reach the wall at Manningtree, what a feast of birds to see
Canada geese take flight in a row so razor-sharp in a line like Red Arrows
Oh there she is, Rosie Red Shank, walking with her red cocktail sticks
Grumpy swans hissing in the wind
Along to the amazing white bridge
Cameron the cormorant stands high on his post with his wings stretched out like a vulture ready to pounce
What a wonderful journey I have in the morning.

Reubin Campbell (12)
St Joseph's College, Ipswich

THE PRIVATE

The private is shaking, so scared to move.
Holding a rifle in his hand,
He will fight for his life and he will fight for his country.
He is saying his last prayer before battle.

He is charging like a storm trooper,
But his face is as white as snow.
He is feeling nauseous, a tear rolling down his face.
He is thinking that he might never see his family again.
This makes his determination increase immensely.

He sees grenades dropping out of the sky,
Like raindrops falling down.
He sees disturbing scenes of people dying.
Telling him to tell his family that he loves them.

Famine is spreading across the country like a bad cold.
The stench of rotting bodies across the trenches.
The ear-piercing sound of gunshots and people screaming
Is enough to bust your eardrums.

He wakes up every morning with bloodstains as red as roses on his coat.
His looks at his gun,
It is rearing to shoot more lead bullets to destroy somebody's life.
Just like him that person would dream to be back with his beloved family,
Doing his normal everyday jobs.
Guns and weapons are evil things, he thought.

The private is shaking.
Thinking to himself will he ever live to hear the bells ring,
But more importantly will he ever see his family.
He must fight for now.

James Fearon (12)
St Joseph's Grammar School, Dungannon

LAST CHANCE

It's been a month, to the day,
Since the ship sailed the other way,
Forced to live like an animal!
If I ever get home, their future is dismal.

But this island is far from man,
I'll just have to get by, if I can.
Wait, what's that? Out on the beach!
With a shrivelled arm I reach…

Smooth like marble, an empty glass bottle!
My mind roars into full throttle.
From this simple thing, I gain so much hope,
Off towards my lair I lope,

To find a scrap of something to write on,
Before this faint last hope is gone.
I grab a stick, and a huge green leaf,
The closest I have to a paper sheaf.

Stick poised, ready to scribble and scrawl
My entire account, I'll write down it all,
Of how I got here, what I've done since,
Although most of it will make me wince

As soon as I've finished, I throw it to the sea,
Full of hope that I'll be found, be set free!
I watch as my last chance floats away,
And I sit down to wait, to wait always…

'Hark! Land ho!' the lookout cries,
I gaze upon paradise with my own eyes!
Emerald, sapphire, shimmering gold!
What adventures, I wonder, will unfold?

A young lad spots something, lying on the beach
A corpse! With all life bleached
From its bones, as it stares into my eyes,
A manic grin on its face, it's covered with flies

Then there's something else, washed up on the beach,
A bottle, with something inside, just out of reach
Of my fingers, so I tip the stuff out,

A story on a leaf, of how this came about.

As I read, a tear comes to my eye.
It was my papa, left here to die.

Claire McCooey (12)
St Joseph's Grammar School, Dungannon

LOVE

As I look across the table
I see his dark gypsy blue eyes
I want to gaze at him for ever
But he has broken my loving smile.

My heart is like a house
That he has not knocked on
There is a river of water between us
That neither of us has crossed.

I still remember the day I saw him
He was joking around with friends
And even though in my head were crossed wires
They straightened out and pointed to him.

As he tugged on my heart strings
I felt I was choking
Only his pure breath could save me
Not one hundred men could stop my dreams about him.

I dream I'm stuck in a black burning room
I'm bound to the wall with no escape
But he chooses the other person to save
My head is full of red smoke.

When I'm with him
It's like travelling at twilight
And in the distance there is a bright light
And as I walk towards it it's the darkness leaving my heart.

Sorcha Drayne (12)
St Joseph's Grammar School, Dungannon

THE DAY THE EARTH STOOD STILL

The day the earth stood still,
It just stood there.
Against its own will,
Among the moon and the stars.
The earth was screaming the death role,
At the huge meteorite heading towards it.
It was as black as coal,
As quick as lightning.

The meteorite was closing in,
Moving at incredible speed.
Soaring through the air bin,
Like a bird without wings.
There was a buzz,
And three more meteorites appeared,
Surrounding Earth from every angle.

Earth was scared,
Of the over-sized pieces of coal.
Like a lion that roared,
The first meteorite attacked-
Only to smash into the second,
Knocking the third off course!
The third hit the fourth at speed,
Boom! as the two meteorites disappeared.
Earth continued doing its daily job,
From that day forward.

Patrick Murray (13)
St Joseph's Grammar School, Dungannon

AUTUMN FALLS

My favourite time of year
When autumn draws near.
As I look out my window I see the leaves fall
I hear a whisper almost as if a call.
The bare branches dance in the wind
As I sat and watched them twirl I grinned.
The nights are dark and eerie
But yet I still find my way to sleep,
In the morning my eyes are bleary.

Open the curtains to a bright sunny day
I couldn't see a thing I have to say.
That cold you would need a winter fleece
A white foggy breath I did release.
The car froze over
The nearly-new Land Rover.
So I go in to boil the kettle
When the whistle has finished I let it settle.

As I think to myself, where has the time gone?
It will be no time to morning and a brand new dawn.
My favourite time of year is no longer here
As winter quickly draws near.

Niamh O'Toole (12)
St Joseph's Grammar School, Dungannon

SAVIOUR

He lay cold and alone.
His surroundings a mystery to his frozen mind.
He tried to stand but he was hurt.
He was reduced to a bloody ball.

He lay afraid: no belongings to be seen.
Who am I? he thought.
Where am I? he pondered.

A bright white light rushed to his aid.
She reached out to him.
She took him in.

He stood up!
No gashes, cuts or bruises.
No blood to be seen.
He walked towards her.

No longer afraid.
No longer alone.

She was his saviour.

Rachel McAllister (12)
St Joseph's Grammar School, Dungannon

MY LITTLE RED SUITCASE

As I unpacked my little red suitcase,
I recalled the amazing holiday we had,
The wonderful things we saw and did,
Just thinking about it makes me feel glad!

Spending precious time with my mum and dad,
And my brothers John and Paul.
But spending time with my granny and granda,
Was the most cherished part of all.

Granny and Granda have told me,
This is the last foreign holiday for them.
It makes me feel so very sad to think,
That next time will be without them.

So as I stand here in my bedroom and begin to unpack
I recall the memories I can never replace.
All these treasures packed inside,
My little red suitcase.

Caitlin McElvogue (12)
St Joseph's Grammar School, Dungannon

BASILISK

I want a mythical snake
Whose fangs are as long as my arm,
Whose gaze is deadly and scales are akin,
To a plate of metal armour.

Whose venom can melt stone stairs,
Who's on the spider's throne,
Whose mother's a chick and
Whose father's a toad.

Whose life blinks out at a rooster's crow,
I want a Basilisk, I do,
A Basilisk, I want.

Oisin McCann (12)
St Joseph's Grammar School, Dungannon

THE BEAUTY THAT LAY UNDER THE MASK

Every day, the same thing lay upon her face,
A mask to cover her fear and depression.

All of her emotions sealed up in a bottle of foundation.
Little did anybody know,
That underneath that thick mask...
Lay a beautiful face,
Like taking a look at a book and judging it,
When inside that book were continuous lines and photographs,
Filled with interesting words and phrases.

But she didn't know this,
And neither did anybody else,
Because she never revealed...
The beauty that lay under the mask.

Aoibheann Christie (12)
St Joseph's Grammar School, Dungannon

THE ENVELOPE

As the clock ticks
I put my pen to paper
And ever word hurts
Just a little bit more!

Every line...
Every word...
Gets more and more dreary
As I write to you!

The envelope
Sealed with my love,
But filled with my tears...
Addressed to the one
I miss the most.

Eva Lamb (12)
St Joseph's Grammar School, Dungannon

GRIEF

Hello sadness, my new friend,
You crept up to me and shook my hand,
As you squeezed my hand so tight my eyes closed to the light.
I feel your lips caress my face, please stop . . . I can't breathe . . . through this embrace.
Please, *no*, I can't let your hand go,
Who are you? Why me? Will I ever be free?

Walking through the aisles again, darkness still holds my hand tight.
I stop and drop my basket to the floor, I can't do this with so little light.
Why is everyone walking past me, not knowing my pain?
I don't want to carry on and be the same, I need someone to blame.
Please stop squeezing my hand, my eyes cloud over and rain drops to the floor.
Who are you? Why me? Will I ever be free?

Will you now always hold my hand?
Could you let go? I shake my head, I know it's no.
I drift through the grass on my way to the past.
I remember you holding my hand and hope the dream doesn't turn to sand,
Still the wind pats my face, reminding me of a warmer embrace,
Who are you? Why me? Will I ever be free?

I move through the day and again get lost on my way,
Friend you can't help me anymore, stop this stalking – it must be against the law.
I'm so alone in this bursting crowd, stop it's just all too loud.
Help isn't far away, I know you're not here to stay.
I now know who you are, and you now know me.
Goodbye pain . . . until we meet again.

Isabelle Alicia Knight (13)
St Luke's Science And Sports College, Exeter

ALL HALLOWS' EVE

Soon it'll be Halloween with ghosts and ghouls,
Children dressing up in costumes acting the fool.
Grandparents screaming when kids shout, 'Boo!'
Children get frightened when the dads join in too.
Moms disappear in a cloud of smoke
Dad and children too think this is some sort of joke.
Dad and children shouting, 'Mom, where have you gone?'
An eerie voice calls out and speaks,
'She's with me, we won't be long!'
A frightened look on their faces,
As they search for mom in different places
Mom calls out the children's names
Peter, Kathy and little James.
'I'm here my children, I'm watching you.'
They look around to find nothing in view
They are scared and frightened as you could expect
But they weren't prepared for what happened next
A crash of thunder and bright flash of light
Mom appeared to give them a fright!

Flannery Shay Umstead (12)
Sanquhar Academy, Sanquhar

MISTY MORNING

Waking up on a misty morning
The hills and trees I cannot see
The sheep and cows I cannot see
But as the sun rises
The mist begins to melt away
Like snow on a sunny day
And as the day begins to brighten up
I can finally see the hills
And trees and cows and sheep
That I could not see before.

Heather Frame (13)
Sanquhar Academy, Sanquhar

PUMPKIN TIME

Pumpkin time is here again,
Time to play trick or treat.
Pumpkin time is here again,
Our spooky friends will meet.

Pumpkin time is great fun,
When you are with your friends,
Go knocking on each door
As you see their scary faces.

Each door has a pumpkin
That represents Halloween,
Go knocking on it
And you'll see you'll get lots of treats.

See the costumes we have on,
Monsters, ghosts, goblins too.
See the costumes we have on,
Hear us all shout, 'Boo!'

Keira Marie Cunningham (11)
Sanquhar Academy, Sanquhar

I HAD A LITTLE PANDA

I had a little panda
Nothing would it eat
But a bamboo stick
And my Uncle Pete.

It chased my little sister
You should have heard her shout
It didn't like my uncle
In fact it spat him out!

Sarah Fisher (11)
Sanquhar Academy, Sanquhar

SKY SONG

The bird, the beautiful bird.
The beautiful winged creature,
Flew through the sky with such freedom.
The freedom that so many now envy.
The freedom that so many had
Until they threw it all away.
Now we're here.
Stuck here,
To decay here.
Till there's no one left here.
Till you and me are gone dear.
Oh the bird,
The beautiful winged creature,
Perfectly crafted,
Every feature.

Rhiannon Flynn (12)
Sanquhar Academy, Sanquhar

SHYNESS POEM

Shyness is purple,
It's like a cold frosty night,
It tastes like dry ice,
It smells like a cold damp house,
Yet, it's soft and can be kind,
It can be encouraging
And make you feel happy
And sometimes relaxed.

Cameron Carter (13)
Sanquhar Academy, Sanquhar

REMEMBER THE FALLEN

All geared up and ready for orders,
The enemy approaches upon our borders,
The air is thick and the tension is black,
Now we're all here we can never turn back.

The orders are given, we're all on the run,
The pounding of hearts and the thunder of guns,
Tanks are everywhere, bodies a blur,
Soldiers lay all around, cold in the dirt.

Four years later, with soldiers a few,
How did we get here? Nobody knew,
So many are hurt, and too many dead,
So we hang up our guns and a truce is then said.

And now every year we remember the lives,
That they gave for our country -
So full of pride.

A poppy we wear to show we remember,
The lives that we lost the 11th November.

Remember the fallen.

Lilli Simmonds
Stour Valley Community School, Clare

THE BALLAD OF CAPTAIN BLACKBEARD

When the wind was a howling gale,
And the sea was rolling death
When the yellow mist came creeping up
With fear in every breath

Out of the empty darkness,
With long black beard aflame
Captain Blackbeard came a-charging
And it wasn't fun and game

The Captain's sword came crashing down,
And he fired his pistol with craze
The dead man lay before him
With a hollow glassy gaze

The other captain shouted out,
He was spinning the broken wheel
His men were fighting for King and country
Armed with the royal seal

Blackbeard's men were doing well,
And the deck was stained with red
With 'Cowards!' shouted at their backs
The King's men turned and fled

He sailed round the many nations,
Shaking tough men's knees
The pirate, Captain Blackbeard
Terror of the seven seas

But in a rundown warship,
They were shaking with aggravation
Their eyes were mad with seething rage
They were discussing assassination.

'I want him dead,' said one man,
'I won't rest till he's died,
I want him killed and killed again.
In his flame he will be fried.'

Then across the misty waters,
In the dead of night

THE POETRY TRIALS - FUTURE VOICES

Came Captain Blackbeard's enemies
Men of towering might

Ding, ding, went the warning bell,
The captain's men had heard it
The pirates leapt right out of bed
Blackbeard and his bandits

The pirates grabbed at every weapon,
The captain lit his beard
They charged out onto the open deck
The figure that everyone feared

At first the battle was going well,
And Blackbeard's men were winning
But then the fight turned for the worst
And Blackbeard's men were thinning

Captain Blackbeard was fighting hard,
But then the man got cornered
And in the faint blue morning light
The pirate legend was murdered

They left him alone on the sinking ship,
The man they knew they'd avenge
Lying alone on the bloody deck
Of the ship Queen Anne's Revenge

But when the wind is a howling gale,
And the sea is rolling death
When the yellow mist comes creeping up
With fear in every breath

Out of the empty darkness,
With long black beard aflame
The ghostly captain will come a-charging
And it won't be fun and game.

Alban Smith-Adams (12)
Stour Valley Community School, Clare

THE REFUGEE

The bullets came flying past my head,
Like a swarm of angry bees,
My mum was screaming my name,
Running and holding the keys.

Children running scared,
Others lying dead,
People running for their lives,
Running from the red.

The old mosque all gone,
Turned into rubble,
Old clothes strewn on the road,
People trying not to stumble.

We keep on walking,
I wonder when we will stop,
I'm sore all over,
Everything's ripped like my top.

We reached the end of the land,
And meet the rolling sea,
I wonder where we are,
Is this where we're meant to be?

My mum said, 'Start swimming.'
I obey like the good boy I am,
Mum is moving ahead of me,
I'm trying as hard as I can.

Everyone starts swimming back,
Mum says, 'Keep going on.'
ISIS is seen on the horizon,
I look for Mum but she's gone.

The dead are floating around me,
One is probably Mum,
Maybe they won't kill me,
No, don't be so dumb.

I wonder if they found my body,
Washed up on the shore,
Maybe people will help,
When they see me no more.

I wonder if they will stop,
I really hope they do,
I really wish they wouldn't kill,
I hope they don't kill you.

Annecy Webb
Stour Valley Community School, Clare

CHERRY BLOSSOM

Climb up the twisted bark,
For a story unravels itself;
As you uncover the blossom's delectable magic
Swelling up into your senses, as you
Breathe in its unforgettable offers.

Or maybe you could express the scent of the blossom
As a miniature water lily perched on a branch,
Or the colour of a milky coffee,
Drenched in fresh cherry juice.

It's still the mother of its pack though
There's no excuse for doubting that,
But even the tree and its cherries have feelings
Of no desperation to be picked for a pie,
However, some day that may eventually come true.

Stories lurk around every corner
But beware, for some shall not ever be uncovered,
Secrets in compact nooks and crannies of the ancient tree
Shall always be locked away forever.

Francesca Blackburn
Stour Valley Community School, Clare

NANNY

It's been a while
But I've missed your smile
I've missed your hugs
And your voice, I'm in denial.

You left so quickly
I couldn't say goodbye
There's been so many tears
All I seem to do is cry.

I remember your necklace
That beautiful gold
It reminds me every day
Until I get old.

The butterfly floats by me
I'm sure it's you
Multicoloured wings
Dancing in the blue.

I miss you.

Jessica Elizabeth McNaul
Stour Valley Community School, Clare

THE SILVER GEM

I can see the moon burning a hole in the noir sky
Brilliant white,
It glows and bleaches all through the night.

Powdery clouds try to cover and dull its beauty
But the light pierces through
It pierces right through me.

Bright dazzling coldness falls onto the shoulders of the weak
Lending a voice, lending a friend
Even when it's bleak
The cries of wolves sooth and excite
As its comforting shimmer conquers the night.

A silver rim of which the light stops
Contrasting on the black
And the shine still carries on, never looking back

The moon is king of all the night parades
Until it silently vanishes when the gem peppered, sky begins to fade.

Morrigan Rimmer
Stour Valley Community School, Clare

THE BLACK SHADOW

Like a lightning bolt in the night
Like a ghost running out of sight
Shadows are thrown away
As it runs till the light of day
On fear, on flight
Till the sun makes its first light
Its evil green eyes stare
It is hard to bear
Is it a beast?
Is it a monster?
A beam of sun was shown.
It glanced at the sun
And then at my eyes
And it fled out of sight
And the black shadow,
Left the night.

Libbie Bush
Stour Valley Community School, Clare

THE BLOOD MOON

It was a night in late September
A full moon was in the sky,
A very special one this time
An eclipse was passing by.
The moon was big, colossal in fact!
They tell me it will not come again
For thirty years or more,
For it was a wonderful moon
That night I saw.
The light from the sun on the moon
Turning it blood-red,
14% bigger than it usually is,
I can't believe this happened
While I was in bed!

Madeleine Jacobs
Stour Valley Community School, Clare

ICE CREAM

A likely reason to involve a cop
Annoyingly it's taken by a thief
A great snack with a cherry on the top
It's cold and refreshing against your teeth.

So many flavours which one do you choose?
At least none of them taste like wood or coal
Try some otherwise you'll miss out – you lose!
Make yourself a fantastic brimming bowl.

No hassle needed there's nothing to bake
If you're quirky this is really cool!
Make it wonderful by adding a flake!
Don't feed it to the birds – eat it you fool!

This extremely fabulous treat does gleam!
Hip hip hooray! Give it up for ice cream!

Lucy Brighton
Stour Valley Community School, Clare

TOMORROW

Black.
That is the colour of the sky today.
Yesterday was black.
The day before that was black.
Every day was black.
The kids at school take pleasure at my pain.
My pain of fear and regret.
The things I did were wrong
And I have to suffer the consequences.
Every day I hope for the better.
For the agony to stop in a wave of relief.
But that day does not come.
I have to suffer because of my past mistakes.
People say there's a tomorrow
But I see none in my future.
I want the burning inside to stop.
This is my way of saying sorry to those I hurt.
But then the sky changed.
I saw light and felt warmth.
I felt happy and full of hope.
I realised one thing.
There is a tomorrow.

Cameron Tyberious Anderson (13)
The Aconbury Centre, Hereford

THE POETRY TRIALS - FUTURE VOICES

A JOURNEY OF REALISATION

A life of fear,
A fear of life,
Not knowing what's to come,
Should I depart from this world?
The wind lay still,
The corn stood still,
The sky looked clear,
The path was empty.
I ran, I ran and I ran.
Stop, now . . .
A voice of an enemy,
A chant of an enemy,
A figure of an enemy.
I ran, I ran and I ran.
The enemy's trace was left behind.
I stop and search.
No food, no water, no shelter,
Just a tear.
One last cry of survival,
I am gone . . .
A harsh awakening,
A chorus of sirens,
I stand up and follow.
Over mountainous hills,
And muddy gorges,
I see the destination,
Unravelling within my vision.
I see a future,
I smell the future,
I am the future.

Madelaine Sanderson (13)
The Kingsley School For Girls, Leamington Spa

BROTHER...

The 30th of the 1st, that's where it went wrong,
For that was when we were told where we belonged.
They shut down our borders,
Our airplanes,
Our lives...
Then I found out what my brother had disguised.
He had left the country, in search of his past,
He never knew that this trip might be his last...
He was locked in America,
Me in Britain.
When the authorities separated us,
They almost looked smitten.
'I have to find him!' I let out with a cry,
Because I knew if I didn't I would surely die.
With all of my courage, I set out on a quest,
To find my brother and let out what I had in my chest.
I ran and I swam, I leaped and I jumped,
Until my wits left me, and I fell down with a crunch.
I'd knocked into guards who were muscular and tall,
'Brother!' I let out with an almighty call.
He was close, I could tell,
Although that was when all noise
Fell...
He lay there unmoving, just a few feet away,
Totally peaceful...
Totally gone...
And so broke my heart,
This world tore me apart,
So now it is time for me to depart...

Helen Lavery (13)
The Kingsley School For Girls, Leamington Spa

THE POETRY TRIALS - FUTURE VOICES

A JOURNEY: UTOPIA OR DYSTOPIA FOR YOU AND ME?

Utopia or dystopia for you and me?
Travelling around by train and track,
From town to country, to city and back,
Life flying by without a care,
Different views are everywhere.

Golden sun, low over an autumn field,
The hazy morning fog hovers gently above,
A lovely fresh scent drifts in and settles.
Heading on, the fog rises dense and dark,
Billowing from chimneys and factories all around,
Suffocating smoke pollutes and blanks out the view.

A carriage full of connecting people,
Marvellous media and social time,
Friends sharing moments, pictures and joy.
But a boy sits alone, thoughtful and sad,
Cyber bullying and fear is all he's had.
Dangerous people post words of hate,
Marvellous media or media madness?

The journey ends at a platform where boards display,
Adverts of perfect people with perfect lives,
'Have it all, anything is possible,' they read.
Whilst the radio reports war, poverty, disasters and more,
And the loss of life, fear and damage soar.
The image shifts in just a moment.
It depends where you look and what you see,
Utopia or dystopia for you and me?

Rebecca Blake (13)
The Kingsley School For Girls, Leamington Spa

NEW YORK

The sun rises in East Brooklyn,
Then the hustle and bustle of city will begin.

The lights of the night begin to fade away,
Vehicles start to invade the highways,
The smell of fresh bagels spreads the street,
Gradually you'll start to feel the sun's heat.

People start to enter the subway,
Some are heading to Broadway,
Now the day has begun,
Everyone can get on with jobs that have to be done.

Tourists start to flood New York Harbour,
Some enter the ice cream parlour,
The boats set off to Staten Island,
You can see it on the horizon.

When the clock strikes 12,
Lunch is delved for,
Central Park is nearly bursting,
With the amount of people inside relaxing.

Nearing to evening,
Workers are leaving,
The lights of the city begin to shine,
Tourists begin to dine.

As the day nears its end,
The late night population gradually descends,
The city that never sleeps is finally quiet.

Gracie Shipley (12)
The Kingsley School For Girls, Leamington Spa

THE POETRY TRIALS - FUTURE VOICES

THE FIRE

The warm flickering,
Of the orange glow,
Its hypnotic power,
Of which no one knows,
The billowing smoke
Floats up to the sky
And ashy sparks
Begin to fly.

Its magical colour,
Forever changing,
The different flames,
Their height exchanging
In an unknown rhythm,
No secrets revealed,
Of its hidden magic,
Its fiery shield.

That is why,
In the dead of night,
In the freezing cold,
You may see a light,
Its billowing smoke,
Floating in the sky,
And its ashy sparks,
Beginning to fly.

Gemma Hotchkiss (12)
The Kingsley School For Girls, Leamington Spa

THE NEW WORLD

Have you ever wondered what a world would be like with no love,
I live in a world where the only love we felt is now a cherished memory with those above.
We were promised the world but now it is non-existent,
The air raids were just too persistent.
The inky midnight sky, timeless from day to night,
It baffles me to think that it used to blanket the Earth with an incandescent starry light.
Jagged skyscrapers like broken jigsaw pieces,
Ebony vegetation weaving between, carrying monstrous diseases.
As April's candle was blustered out, flurrying into May,
There was no sign of spring, just dismal dismay.
They called it the New World but all children know is death and destruction.
Looming, meandering pavements maze around, leading to gangs and abduction.
A constant sixth sense tingles up my spine of colossal air ships skulking the skies.
A society where all humans are told treacherous lies.
I am not a human, I am a number.
Peace and love is in a heavy slumber.
There is no equality just a staggering hierarchy,
I live in a societyless society.

Annie Harper Radley (13)
The Kingsley School For Girls, Leamington Spa

VENICE

Landing on the runway,
Here we go – the first day
Waiting for my luggage,
Takes too long, I buy a beverage.
Got my bags, now to the bus,
Why is this trip such a fuss?
Off the bus and on a boat,
The wind is sharp, even with my coat.
My adrenalin,
Starts to kick in,
A walk into town,
Small, petite streets to go down,
Turn and see the Rialto Bridge,
This is no way a wreckage,
I'm a tourist, lots to see,
But most important is something for me,
How about a scoop of ice cream!

Lucie Jones (12)
The Kingsley School For Girls, Leamington Spa

THE AIR WAS COLD AND CRISP

The air was cold and crisp,
The world small and bliss.
Not all was lost and forgotten;
What's been seen should never be forgotten.
Torture from within withholds the empty streets.
We've been cornered and slaughtered,
Beaten and conquered.
Five years ago they said it would improve,
This was soon known to not be true.
Through the wind and hollowing weights,
I have met life's horrible dates.
The day of that was known to this,
The air was cold and crisp.

Helena Mannion (14)
The Kingsley School For Girls, Leamington Spa

A WALK TO SEE MY BROTHER

I leave my house on a cold dark day,
It's autumn time, the leaves have turned grey,
I go down the hill and breathe in the fog,
I enter the wood, climb over the dead log,
The path is narrow with the brambles encroaching,
I kick my way through and feel the thorns choking,
The usual smell reminds me a dog has been past,
So my pet is excited but that won't last,
I pass through a gate that's all knocked down,
The sign is all rusty, the catch is all brown,
The lake shines black, the reeds are like sticks,
The duck swims past without any chicks,
I lift up my head in search of my brother,
I see a dark shape but it is another,
My excitement is raised as I enter the park,
But he is not there, everything's dark.

Shakirah Saquhlan (13)
The Kingsley School For Girls, Leamington Spa

DYSTOPIA: DEATH

- D : The dark of the future will start creeping upon you. Get used to it whilst you can . . .
- E : You feel enraged, why am I here? You ask yourself. Ideas are spinning around your head about what is happening to you every second and every minute. You won't let yourself believe one of them.
- A : You've been abducted to a world you feel like you're drowning in and you know there's no way out from now.
- T : Torment, it's all you know. You eventually get used to the feeling of tears streaming down your face from the pain you constantly feel.
- H : Your breathing has become heavy from the horrid, harsh air you continue to breathe in that's dragging on your lungs, weighing you down.

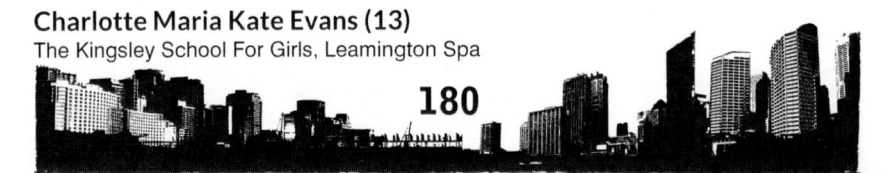

Charlotte Maria Kate Evans (13)
The Kingsley School For Girls, Leamington Spa

AILING AMERICA

After the revolution,
After Grandfather became king,
The united districts of America changed,
He didn't let me and Jason with the others,
We couldn't love civilians,
Only the other royals,
But then he came along,
I really love him,
I sacrificed my crown and my family,
But he left me for an easier life,
Free,
I'm joining him now,
Goodbye,
I love you,
A single tear fell.

Jenna Kate Morgan (13)
The Kingsley School For Girls, Leamington Spa

DEATH IS OUT

There is no law,
Only survival,
Evil walks on the Earth now,
Hell is out.

People wondered how,
But now there are no people to wonder,
Animals are dying,
But now there are no animals to die.

The only thing on Earth,
The only thing at all,
Are the oceans of blood,
And the bodies of the people.

Lily Constance (13)
The Kingsley School For Girls, Leamington Spa

THE VAMPIRE

Inside the vampire's fang, the deep dark mountain.
Inside the deep dark mountain, the vampire's skin.
Inside the vampire's skin, the red blood of a human.
Inside the red blood of a human, the vampire's mouth.
Inside the vampire's mouth, the shrieks of its prey.
Inside the shrieks of its prey, the vampire's sneer.
Inside the vampire's sneer, the flesh of its prey.
Inside the flesh of its prey, the vampire's white face.
Inside the vampire's white face, the human's bronze eyes.
Inside the human's bronze eyes, the vampire's sharp eyes.
Inside the vampire's sharp eyes, the crystal lake.
Inside the crystal lake, the vampire's fang.

Harkeiran Sohal (13)
The Kingsley School For Girls, Leamington Spa

HIM

His vocals, I could absorb for days
A million yards from the point at which it plays
His willow orbs sparkling from the bright sky
Slowly clouding, at the hurtful words, starting to cry
Looking up at the mass of fans jumping, singing his songs
Upon the platform the boy should stay all along
The show has passed, just him in his room
Thinking about the last two hours, his vision following the ivory moon
Flashbacks of beautiful days unfold in his mind
Causing his lips to shift
Showing off an outstanding grin, all too kind

His charm could win a girl's soul
A day with him, not at all dull.

Though our paths won't cross
My wish will stay
Knowing you're happy is worth the wait.

Annie Lynch (13)
The Thetford Academy, Thetford

THE BEAR

I sat in the chair,
Across the room was a bear,
Giving me a dim and dismal stare.

The bear stood up,
Looked me in the eyes,
And walked away,
I was surprised.

Through the back door,
In a cabin far away,
Came an old man,
Who had had a busy day,

He slumped down in his seat,
Waiting for something to eat,
After trying to clean his smelly feet.

The next day he and his wife had a squabble,
His eyes were all wrinkled and started to wobble,
Tears slowly dripped and fell on the cobble.

He left an hour later,
His suitcase all packed,
His wife looked out the window,
And then she cracked,
'Oh husband, come home please!'
She bent down and began to plead on her knees,

There was no turning back.

The old man walked as far as he can,
He finally came to a train station.

After buying his tickets he sat on a chair,
Across the room there was a bear,
Giving him a dark and dismal stare.
His wife was no longer there.

Spencer Hornsby (13)
The Thetford Academy, Thetford

A SUMMER FOR EVERYONE

An espy of the glistening sun catches my eye
On an early summer's morning,
The last day of school is approaching
Everything seems to be blooming.

As the freezing, creamy, glutinous ice cream
Sticks to my face like glue
I remember that this season isn't the season of flu
This is a summer for everyone.

I feel like this is the season I adore the most
Beaches, sandcastles near to the coast
Surfing and summer fun
My holiday has just begun
This is a summer for everyone.

Fish and chips by the shore
Sand instead of wooden floor
Water washing onto my feet
People dancing to the beat
This is a summer for everyone.

I miss how things were before
Wooden floor instead of sand
In my bedroom listening to my favourite band
Roast dinner instead of chips
Watching whole programmes instead of clips
I watch the moon go down at night
That was a perfect summer for everyone!

Elise Smith (13)
The Thetford Academy, Thetford

THE VOLUNTEER

She was the volunteer,
The first in centuries,
Sacrificing herself for her sister.

As a tear rolled down her cheek,
She moved one step towards her death,
She felt one second pass and there she was,
Standing . . . no choice, can't turn . . .

She was panic-stricken,
She winced, aghast at the cruelty,
Seconds left until final countdown . . .

She looked down
She got ready
Steady
Beep . . . !
She ran as she saw people expire,
She climbed up a tree, as high as possible,
Peter! The betrayer!
He's teamed with the people from other districts!

They spotted her on that tree, her heart
Stopped.
They waited under the tree she was on,
Then she saw her, the girl!
She pointed at the branch with dangerous bees,
That's when we got the idea!

Michaela Matasova (13)
The Thetford Academy, Thetford

LIFE

Life has no definition,
Choices and decisions,
That lead to your destination.

Every soul is unique,
Some are able to speak,
Victory or defeat.

An ocean, calm and still,
Or rough and raging,
In the end,
Always beautiful.

Like a tree with leaves,
Some fall,
Some stay,
Like fire can cause war or peace.

Used and wasted,
Abused and hated,
Others,
Loved and wanted,
Cherished and adored.

Fights and scars,
Ups and downs,
Are you prepared for the journey?

Annabel Phillips (12)
The Thetford Academy, Thetford

STEP ON!

Emotions overwhelming
The only time to go or turn . . .
My mind is saying,
Point toes, straight knees!

Keep smiling,
Stay on top!

One second left,
One choice . . .

I feel the music getting through my body,
It gets my muscles move,
Like I'm somebody's doll.

One move, the other
Goes well for now,
The judges look at me like everything is wrong
But I'm the only one who knows the right.

The end . . .

Now everyone is waiting,
You close your eyes and . . .

Cheer

You won, you got what you deserve!

Sofija Zurba (12)
The Thetford Academy, Thetford

SOCIAL ANXIETY

Social phobia
Trapped in a cage of my own
Self-doubting despair.

Genesis Baker (15)
The Thetford Academy, Thetford

FOOTBALL IS LIFE

Football is football,
Football is life,
Football is great, it should be a part of your life,
Football is great,
Football is life,
You can get tackled, that's not quite as fun,
Football is passion,
Football is life,
I once cried because I had no football boots, that's not all right,
Football is splendid,
Football is life,
One day I got football boots and that's where it began,
Football is football,
Football is life,
I started playing when I was 4, out of nowhere Ronaldo knocks at my door,
Football is great,
Football is life,
Ronaldo – a professional football player oh what a surprise,
Football is passion,
Football is life,
Ronaldo taught me a lot, now I'm on my way to be with a professional team...

Kieran Dixon (12)
The Thetford Academy, Thetford

BLACK

Black, the colour of death,
The shade of the Reaper's robe,
Frankenstein's monster's hair.
Also the colour of a squid's ink,
Tar is black as coal.
The most expensive tuxedos,
A goth's favourite tint.

Cory Jay Thomas (13)
The Thetford Academy, Thetford

GRANDAD

My granddad was the best,
He made us laugh,
He fixed everything,
From lights to electronics,
It was very sad when he passed,

Except he isn't in pain now,
He loved his Mars bars,
He had a full jar of them,

My granddad was very special,
Even though he was in pain,
I like the thought of being in a plane,
Because I feel closer to him,

My granddad didn't live very long,
It was sad to find out he passed,
Because it left a hole inside,

I miss my granddad so much,
When I think of him I cry,
I miss you granddad,
For ever in our hearts.

Libby Donno (11)
The Thetford Academy, Thetford

THE PERFECT PARADISE

It's a place we can relax, nothing but excitement.
It's a getaway to a place with a tonne of sun.
Diving in the refreshing sea.

It's the only place I want to be.

Palm trees swaying in the soft and gentle breeze.
Golden sand between my toes.
All together the ocean – the true show.

In the night the sparkling lights, they shine so bright . . .

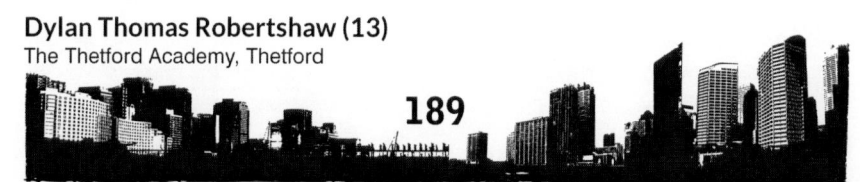

Dylan Thomas Robertshaw (13)
The Thetford Academy, Thetford

WHO AM I?

Though I'm laughing outwardly, I'm crying within,
Trying not to show how much pain I am in.
Hiding my sorrow, putting on a show,
Not allowing anybody to know.
Standing solitary in shadows so dark,
My chalky skin against such black, a contrast that is stark.
My wrists as thin as twigs, my nails cut and torn,
Partitioning my body from nights so cold – rags both cut and worn.
You don't know who I am, you know nothing of my past,
For good things do not stay for long, good things do not last.
My soul is an obscurity, my spirit has no aim,
'What am I?' you might ask, but this is all I can proclaim:
I am an unsaid thought; until now not told,
I am not fat or thin or young or old.
I am a nobody, for body I own not,
I am that which is always forgot.
Knowing who I am is a thing you cannot do,
But though that is right, I can still know you.
I know your sorrow, I know your pain, I know what you go through,
'Who am I?' you might ask, I am only you . . .

Leigh Mortimer (14)
The Thetford Academy, Thetford

OVERCOMING CANCER MUM!

You overcome cancer Mum
I see you burn
Once you burn off cancer
You run off like a real woman
Up and down roads all day
Finding your way
Being all new
I know cancer brought you down
You're up again on your legs
A crazy hour now!

Caitlin Gray (11)
The Thetford Academy, Thetford

BEST FRIENDS

I've got your back, you've got mine
I'll help you out anytime.
To see you hurt, to see you cry
Makes me weep and want to die.
And if you agree to never fight
It wouldn't matter who's wrong or right.

Here you are, I am here
Today's the day we'll scream and cheer
When you are as funny as a clown
You turn my frown upside down
You get me food and get me drink
When I forget, you make me think
How lucky I am to have you.

Now we have to leave and go back home
The day is gone, another story to be told
But I'm so sad to see you go
I hope we have a fun time in the snow
We make great things and make a great team
I'll see you soon, just never forget me.

Dylan Kirk (11)
The Thetford Academy, Thetford

A SCHOOL'S DAY

I go to an outstanding school in an outstanding town.
It has amazing classrooms with astonishing staff.
Joyful, outstanding class, to learn anything you want.

With a gigantic chain of kids waiting for lunch,
Amazing hot food and all sorts of rolls.

I'm liking this school,
School days finish mainly at 3:45
And pupils jump for joy
For a hard day's work.

Georgia Shannon Tosney (11)
The Thetford Academy, Thetford

AMAZING ANIMALS

Drifting away from day and night
Animals start to run out of sight
Back again for careful days
Whilst huntsmen hop far away

Lions growl at hunting packs
Hippos join unhappy fans
Humans hungry for yummy pig
But animals hiding down in a dip

Humans strong, proud and all
Think it's a fun game but no
If you chop animal skin
No animal shall win

Killing grounds not a good tool
Amazing animals in the world
Don't kill for fun, no, no, no
Don't be unfair
Amazing animals
You should know.

Madison Lorraine Brunec (11)
The Thetford Academy, Thetford

I AM ...

I am Lyddle Diddle Wonky
Lyddle Diddle is my way,
I am clumsy and I'm tall,
But this is how I'm cool.

I may walk into doors,
And fall onto floors,
Trip up stairs,
And fall on chairs.

I am Lyddle Diddle Wonky,
And this is how I'm cool!

Lydia Dixon (11)
The Thetford Academy, Thetford

MY DOG

I love my dog
Her name is Buffy
A Labrador retriever
Black flowing fur waving in the wind
As the sun beats down on her
Majestic footsteps flicking up the dirt
As she zooms across the mossy green field
Shining in the sun
As black as night
See her shadow speed past the street light
The loud bark echoes in the silence
Hear the rustle of the bushes
As muntjacs run past my feet
She never stops running
She's always protective to me and my brother
She is very playful to one another
When she gets home
She goes to her bed
To get her energy there's a new day ahead.

Jordan Valentine (11)
The Thetford Academy, Thetford

MUSIC

Music is a soft tune that you listen to
Music is something that calms you down
Something that makes you happy
Something that you listen to all the time
It sometimes makes you happy, it sometimes makes you sad
It sometimes makes you wonder what if that was real life?
But sometimes you listen to it and you don't even realise
That this is not real life
This is only an imaginative world that you listen to all the time
It's only a sweet dream
That fairies fly in a bright blue sky . . .

Kotryna Miliskeviciute (13)
The Thetford Academy, Thetford

DANCE

Is it a mystery that it's my love?
It could make my mind blow.
It's like life, every mistake might ruin it,
You never know how it might affect your soul.
What about us, what about dreaming?
Dance is the opposite of it all.
Whenever we do it, we can make it clearer,
We can wait, till the end of the world
But dance is all of my love.
It's inside of my heart, inside of my mind
Nothing will change it; it's just the way I look on the world.

Whatever you're going to do it would never change,
Contemporary: mine and the only one.
It makes me feel better not worse,
Doesn't it sound weird? It probably does.

Improvisation makes it more fun,
You can change the way it is shown,
But it will still be the best of it all.

Wiktoria Bialek (13)
The Thetford Academy, Thetford

WINTER FLAKES

White as a snowflake, clouds
Pure white above my head,
Like candyfloss, look above
White shiny stars, white
Corpses pale white, due to the
Reflection of all visible rays of light
Colour of the sheep's wool.
Looking at the clouds like heaven has
stumbled upon me.

Tomas Diogo (13)
The Thetford Academy, Thetford

GROWING BUSH

Bush, turning brown
Kids start to frown
As sun was warm
But now it's torn apart
What is this form?
Autumn, autumn, autumn, autumn.

Oh bush, turning gold
This is what kids got told
Adults say, 'Cold is time
To wrap up warm.'
What is this cold form?
Autumn, autumn, autumn, autumn.

Small bush, tiny, starting to grow, no!
Now it's starting to snow!
Snow is starting to fall.
I wish I was told this kind of form.
'Now what form is starting?' kids said.
'Just wait, just wait,' said the adults.

Jessica Hendricks (11)
The Thetford Academy, Thetford

MARSHMALLOW SKY

Happy as I can be, my dreams came true!
All of the clouds came together to celebrate!
All of a sudden the clouds became whiter than petals from a daisy.
The clouds became one!
All of these random edges became as soft as cotton!
Least expected, the cloud split into two!
The second cloud became as pink as Minnie Mouse's dress.
I wish I could reach the marshmallow sky!
And eat a whole mouthful!

Aleksandra Jaworska (12)
The Thetford Academy, Thetford

THE AGES

Now underneath our very feet
Are the giant skeletal remains of great beasts.
Beasts that fought for food, fought for water
Died as the Earth got hotter and hotter
They were polished off by a giant rock in the sky
Believe me, I'm not the one to lie
After them came people and big woolly beasts
And ice and snow came with them
Diseases swept the place,
The woolly beasts died and the people stayed to travel
And innovate in the world,
They travelled to different worlds
And the supernatural was left to roam the worlds
They overtook and the world went dark,
All this innovation and concentration was useless.
When the supernatural ruled the world.

Abbie-Lee Stevens (12)
The Thetford Academy, Thetford

THE POETRY TRIALS - FUTURE VOICES

A WARM NIGHT

The warmth of the night
The reflection of the moon
As it glistens in the pond
Whilst the pitter-patter of the
Rain settles you down as
You take the last sip of
Your hot chocolate before
Falling into a magical, dreamy
Sleep . . .

The bubble you fly away in
The pipe in the sky
The dreams that make you
Feel special, the ones that make you
Feel like you can
Fly . . .

Kellesha Brown (12)
The Thetford Academy, Thetford

NICK DUNNE'S POINT OF VIEW

(Based On The Book 'Gone Girl')

12pm
Grey is an unsettling colour,
I turned that colour the day she disappeared.
I loved her.
She'd always seemed so kind, but she wasn't what she appeared.
Amy, what have you done?

Two days gone.
How can this be?
It seems like our marriage is done,
You were like a mermaid that came up from the sea.
I loved her.
What do I do now?

Molly Victoria O'Brien (14)
The Thetford Academy, Thetford

OUT OF THIS WORLD

O utstanding
U niverse
T hroughout

O ur
F amilies and friends

T he nature
H ow it's so pretty
I t fills the world with light
S o silently it dances, spreading its joy

W orldwide it travels
O ver every country
R ivers flow
L ike never before
D reaming of having the time of their lives.

Takitha Marie Malkinson (11)
The Thetford Academy, Thetford

THE POETRY TRIAL

T op of the border
H eading for the win
E very part in order

P utting it into place
O ver left and right
E veryone knows my case
T ill the middle of the night
R eally I think I'm going to ace
Y et my words are going out of sight

T houghtlessly writing
R eaching the goal
I nside I'm fighting
A ll of it feels like a troll
L eaping like lightning.

Jack Thompson
The Thetford Academy, Thetford

THAT MEAN BULLY!

I hate that bully,
But she doesn't understand fully,
She bullies me daily,
We all fear her, very.

She is a witch
Has a twitch,
Her magic house should not be feared,
Even though it hasn't let out a single tear!

Her black cat
Turns human
Her little pet
It's cute and attracts you
But when you least expect . . .
Miaow!

Iris Da Silva (11)
The Thetford Academy, Thetford

THE RAINBOW POEM

The glorious, majestic rainbow.
See it's beautiful
Exotic, neon, natural colours glimmer
And sparkle in the hot
Oak tree, orange sunlight.

When you find the sparkling
Dazzling, jaw-dropping golden cauldron full of gold
Then watch the funny, red-cheeked
Always-jolly leprechaun
Go sliding along the rainbow
Coming to congratulate you
On finding the gold
Lying at the end of the rainbow.

Drew Chapman (11)
The Thetford Academy, Thetford

A FLASH BACK

This is a flashback, too scary, too horrible,
You will be hit by a cold air,
You sprint to a chair,
Trying to stay out of sight,
Soon you think a burglar isn't far away,
You walk downstairs, not making a sound.
Poof!

It was just you all along,
You climb upstairs,
Taking a look out of the window,
You go to nap,
Still now a flashback from that night
Haunts you!

Sharika-Lee Francis (11)
The Thetford Academy, Thetford

HOMELAND

Verdant land, as only a place of silence,
Place with no people, place with no violence.
Where nothing is as it is seen,
Where every human's lost in dreams.
Where young and old is the same age,
There were is evil caught in cage.
Strength of mind, which have that seen?
Human want to lead that place,
But nature is their queen!
Where is that place of calm existence?
Where is that peaceful land?
Where is that place of brave resistance?
It is my Homeland!

Vladislav Bandy (14)
The Thetford Academy, Thetford

THE POETRY TRIALS - FUTURE VOICES

SAY NO TO RACISM

We all must bring racism to an end,
A message to all, I long to send.
The colours of the world all join as one,
This is how it should have been since Earth had begun.
Black, white and brown, we're all the same,
Colour won't matter ever again.
Religions, countries or even names,
Doesn't have a single change to anyone!
This is the debt I pay,
Just for one hard day.
Years of regret and belief,
Sorrow without relief.

David Goncalo Ferreira (12)
The Thetford Academy, Thetford

PURPLE

The flavour of blackcurrant
Running down your throat
Magical glistening colour
Royal as could be
Pretty little violets
Covering my lawn.

Royal Emperors showing
Off their gowns
The smell of lavenders
Fresh as could be
Silky, bright elegant
What's more to say?

Layla Lloyd (12)
The Thetford Academy, Thetford

FRIENDSHIP

No one knows what this is like
No one understands
Because this can hurt
And hurt so much
Behind this mask
No one can see
That you and me could just be free
I just wish we could rewind
And turn back time
Because we need this
We need this so much
To start again and just be friends.

Vera Morgado (11)
The Thetford Academy, Thetford

THY GLOOM

Thy gloom is a cataract of downpour, constant.
It is a pain no human can withstand.
It grasps you by thy talus with no warning.
It transports thy numb and frigid.
It is a district of thy solitary,
But this is only thy casing of this anguish.
Thy shadows hold a thousand myths.
Till this day a calamity is worth an outlandish amount of words.
Thy blood is as thick as thy flowing branch.
No rays of gold bask in thy luminosity shining through thy billow of vapour.
But only this monstrosity can ruin our vitality.

Dianne Jayne Wood (13)
The Thetford Academy, Thetford

LONE LOVE

Fresh start, first sight
Heartbeat, bleak and lonely
Silence crying, while waiting
Lone love – a word for such a feeling.

Dusty shelves, pure empty heart
Fingers didn't touch their spine for long.
Everyday reflection appearing in the window
Library standing there like a lonely single tree.

Playground they notice, library everyone avoids
No life, the books read themselves
Is someone here to bring inspiration back?

Claudia Fernandes (14)
The Thetford Academy, Thetford

MY DOG

She jumps in the boiling sun
And is always fun
She has the heart of a million people
And is incredibly lovely.

I throw the ball and
She chases it like
A wasp flying like lightning to its hive

She has a beautiful smile
Grinning her teeth like she's
Done something bad
She is my dog.

Shaun Green (11)
The Thetford Academy, Thetford

ANIMAL LIPOGRAM

(Lipogram – T)

Deep, deep in Africa a proud lion lay soaking up sun,
Along came a cheeky monkey looking for fun,
'Come and play, come and play,' Cheeky Monkey said,
'All you ever do is lay in your bed!'

Lazy Lion shook his head, 'Go away Cheeky
Or I'll knock off your head.'
Cheeky screeched and ran away,
'I will never ever be your prey.'
Cheeky ran in search of fun
While Lazy Lion soaked up sun.

Jessica Norkett (12)
The Thetford Academy, Thetford

A SWAN'S TALE

A bright majestic bird ready to unleash its beauty on the river floor.
Flowing and feasting away at its golden delight.
Showing off its gorgeous and its whitened wings.
Jealousy flowing like a virus through the blood of the citizens.
Feeling the urge to do anything they can to end that swan of great power.
Swans gone neither in a good place or a bad place.
The time of the swan had come to end with terror and regret.

Joshua Plumley (12)
The Thetford Academy, Thetford

THE POETRY TRIALS - FUTURE VOICES

SHY GIRL

The shy girl walked into her classes,
She wore her uniform and her black glasses,
Sitting in the classroom alone,
Not moving a bone.

She was afraid
Of the mistakes she made
She was scared of her life.

Chloe Crick (14)
The Thetford Academy, Thetford

THE MONSTER (EVERY DAY)

I have to pretend there's nothing wrong,
Act like nothing's happened, and stay strong.
My brain isn't too clear, and my thoughts start to veer
And before you know it, I'm stuck, in the closet: queer.

Slowly as you wait in the dark for the right day to let it out,
Your own brain begins slowly to doubt,
And the monster that is your own head
Begins to wonder if you'd rather be dead.

Yes, some will grind you down,
But all you can do is suck it up and wear a frown.
Your own mind gives you the label
'Faggot' or 'Bender', and it's so painful
You want to finish the torment you own mind creates
Because in your mind, you think, you have no 'mates'

That monster that is *your own* brain
Begins doubting again, and makes you insane.
And the fear that devours your only positivity
Takes away your only ability
To ever be happy again, and leaves you ashamed all of the time
Feeling isolated – as if you've committed the most terrible crime.

The thing some fail to understand
Is that sometimes there's no one there to lend a hand
But the monster in your head goes on ravaging,
And the questions in your mind keep asking.

But you have to go on, living your life
Because at the end of the day, no one's worried about your strife.
It's just something about you – being gay.
You can go on happy, *proud* and carefree – every day.
Because the only thing really stopping you getting stronger
Is your own mind: the beast, the monster.

Ryan Gooderham (15)
Thurston Community College, Bury St. Edmunds

INSPIRE

Believe you can achieve,
The girl who cries herself to sleep,
You could be the one to speak.
Remember your friend people hate,
Prove to them he's a good mate.
Be there to help,
Make people feel great.
A kind word or two,
Could save a life.
A smile on a face makes you great.
Save a life,
Yes you,
Someone will look up,
And say, 'I didn't give up, because of you,'
You are their inspiration,
A hero,
No cape,
But love and faith.
'Can I help?'
Could save another life,
People deserve life,
Don't let them give up,
Be nice,
Help,
Be a hero,
Inspire,
Not be the fire!
Love and aspire.

Emily Robyn Lane
Trinity Education Centre, Trowbridge

WICKED INCURSIONS

I heard a whisper on my shoulder;
Their breath as cold as winter's ice.
Relax now, you've reaped your reward.
I just hope that it would suffice.

Just know that I must go now
And not a day shall pass that I don't think of you.
Your courage, your kindness, your aura of serenity.
My only wish, 'We shall meet again.'

What is that over yonder?
A scythe submerged in ravenous grass.
Bathed in blood, stained with red.
His or mine it wouldn't matter.
We already live in a dark world, a desolate world.
The skies have already blackened enough.

But you will come to the end of the Earth,
And you will find me waiting there.
Where the gates of Hell are bent over and rusted,
You will find my name carved inside.
Just know that in your final hours, with your final breath,
When you're old and grey just know that there is still hope for us again.

Hope that motivates us, hope that drives us.
Hope to see the golden glow again.
Hope to stop the dying of the light.

Lewis Moreton (15)
University Technical College Norfolk, Norwich

CHINESE EDUCATION

Books and books
I can't keep up
Knowledge filling my brain
My grades are up
So I am in good luck
Explore more facts
I need more time to relax
I study for 15 hours a day
Knowledge is my life
And it's something that I like
This is my life in China as a Chinese student.

Georgia Immins (13)
Uppingham Community College, Oakham

THE MIDNIGHT FOX

Dark, dull and dingy buildings,
Ascending walls, towering ceilings.
No sanctuary, no sight of home,
Always moving, forever alone.
Hooves sound and hounds bark,
Running, running in the dark.
A shotgun sounds, bullets go,
The scarlet blood begins to flow.
Limping, limping, one more step,
Persevering, yet still a wreck.
Dead end, suddenly trapped,
Sadistic laughs, claps and claps.
Screaming, yelling, shouting into the void
In its heart, his mother's cries.
Eyes roll back, blood goes cold,
'Don't let them catch you' he was always told.
Succumbing to the pain, memories return to he,
The bright, blinding light appears, the midnight fox is free.

Jasmine Chanian (13)
Wolverhampton Grammar School, Wolverhampton

A DEEP DARK DREAM

A deep dark dream.
One that seems to last forever.
I can't tell anyone.
Whatsoever.

I can't show my emotions,
My feelings I have to confide.
It's harder than you think
To keep it inside.

I want to open up and cry,
But I can't even do that.
The darkness consumes me,
Like an abyss of velvet black.

I'm getting used to being lonely,
My own thoughts for company.
If only I could tell them,
But it stays in my custody.

They don't know that I can hear them,
All the things that they have said,
I always remember,
Lying here in this bed.

I want to go now,
End this eternal dream.
It's always been like this,
Black: the theme.

This wasn't just a dream,
It doesn't seem to end,
This was a coma,
That just seemed to impend.

I feel so alone.
It's hard for me to cope.
I want to go now,
But I can always hope . . .

Brandon Taylor (12)
Wolverhampton Grammar School, Wolverhampton

THE WAR WITHIN

Death doesn't scare me,
Not anymore.
I've long been expecting it,
My body's at war.
My cells are mutating,
There's nothing I can do.
They're running out of treatments,
My days are now few.
I feel the light,
Drawing me in.
Closer and closer,
Comes the monster within.
My body's not my own anymore,
The devil inside is winning.
The race toward a prolonged life,
Is slowly and steadily leaving.
As this bitter civil war,
Gets bigger and bigger inside me.
My spirit, getting crushed,
Is withered and dead already.
I desperately look to my mum,
To end my losing battle.
She simply smiles and holds my hand,
As my lungs continue to rattle
I look to the drips,
Attached to my body.
I want to pull them out,
That would make me happy.
My mechanical lungs constrict and constrain,
As the drips continue to drain.

Caelan Ferguson (14)
Wolverhampton Grammar School, Wolverhampton

BEDTIME STORIES

The emptiness teased me,
Darkness beckoned me closer,
Temptation was overwhelming.
Capturing me in its enclosure.

It's hard to resist,
The eternal night.
Like a velvet cloak,
It swept over me without a fight.

Great myths are just tales of venom,
Legends are knives poised to attack.
Bedtime stories are a form of poison.
All stories with imagination that lack.

The world is just an illusion.
All that's real, is death and destruction.
The only life I've known consists of betrayal.
Life as we know it is just a production.

Don't give in to the darkness,
Fight back against sleep,
Don't listen to the bedtime stories
They will make you weep.

Oliver Brookes (11)
Wolverhampton Grammar School, Wolverhampton

FLAT 22

Staring up at her concrete prison,
You're trapped with her.
Minds connected, you feel her pain. And it hurts.
Pushing the door open, it answers with a creak,
Welcoming deserted hallways greet you.
But behind closed doors, people live in their own s***;
No one cares. I've given up too.
Stairs or lift?
Stairs.

Footsteps echo around, the sound bouncing off the bare walls.
Every step takes you closer.
Stained carpets providing variation from the bland walls,
Needles, smashed glass, glint in the yellow light,
Evidence. But not unusual, not here.

This is her floor, it's only her up here,
No one else would compromise.
She thrives on her own company.

She opens the door
She won't smile at you
Through her empty eyes
All hope drained.
Her thin hair, bruised hands.
She's still sane.

She wants you to stay
And you stare out the closed window
Already yearning to leave.
In every room, her heavy breath,
She follows, like the carpet smell.
She suffers.
Flat 22.

Henry Phillips (15)
Wrekin College, Wellington

INPATIENT – MENTAL HEALTH AWARENESS

Rocking. Rocking. Rocking.
Tears rolling down their sun-deprived, chalk-white cheeks -
Slowly rocking . . .

Rocking like a rocking horse
Captured by anxiety for the inevitable future -
Yet, forever hallucinating the traumatic past.

Minds taking tangential twists;
Lurching deep down into the mud and sleet.
Rather than fighting their thoughts' daily routine -
They'd soon be leaping off a cliff.

Staying in an environment full of irrational people
With monsters consumed inside their feeble heads;
Too dangerous to live in the wilderness,
Too innocent to be dead.

Away from home for too long this environment can seem like reality,
Turning patients into friends -
Too scared, too lonely to shed a tear.
Spending their time unconsciously mixing fate with reality -
Praying to become extinct. Gone.

Re-reading letters from loved ones,
Wishing they would be here;
To say goodbye to their angels
To kiss away their fear.

Professionals dominate their time trying to convince
Them how they feel is wrong. Insane. An imbecile.

Alarm bells shriek every night, which causes nothing but chaos and fear
The others can do nothing but hug themselves to sleep,
Keeping precious possessions near . . .

THE POETRY TRIALS - FUTURE VOICES

These abandoned children I have encountered,
They are honest, pain-stricken people I shall never forget. I believe
Scars and wounds tell a story – a story of an individual -

A story which isn't over yet . . .

Becky Woolley (15)
Wrekin College, Wellington

THE MIND GRABBER!

I was strolling through the park,
And I felt a breath on the back of my neck!
I looked each way
But no one was there
The leaves moved,
No other life was around
Then it came again
What should I do?
No one can help!

Again,
I felt the breath but this time it was icy,
What should I do?
All I could see were trees and a children's playground . . .

But there behind me out of the shadow of the tree
Was neither a man nor an animal,
It was just a figure of orange that lit up the darkness of the night sky!

It started to walk towards me opening up its mouth,
Suddenly it put its arms out and slowly edged my way!
I started to run but tripped on the kerb,
Coming closer, I started to shiver, then started to back away
I jumped and ran then suddenly the road ended with a bush!
It gained on me then all I could see was darkness;
It had put me in its mind!
What should I do?
My life, is it over?
Is this where everything ends?

Isabelle Driscoll (11)
Wrekin College, Wellington

FIREWORKS

We look up at the sky,
It's dark; as black as coal.
We hold our breath and wait
For the fireworks to explode.

Everyone waits in silence
As the men work behind the fence.
You can sense the tension
As the show is about to commence.

Then suddenly a *bang!*
A squeal, a *whee*, a *whizz*,
As the fireworks burst into life
With a *pop*, a *zoom*, a *fizz*.

They blast off like rockets,
They shoot across the sky,
They shatter into a million pieces
And rain down from up high.

Some dance and twist and spin,
Some race and reach the moon,
While others carpet the sky
Like snowdrops in full bloom.

The night is full of colour,
Like a Jackson Pollock painting.
The sky's a perfect canvas
For this multicoloured lightning.

And now for the finale
The crowd all clap and cheer.
They always save the best till last
Can't wait until next year!

Annie Grimsdale (11)
Wrekin College, Wellington

DAD

When I sat by your hospital bed,
Could you feel me?
When I said 'please don't go,'
Why could you not agree?
I can feel you leaving us here in this room,
Slowly, quietly, as the bustle of life outside carries on.

The light is dimmed and the curtains are drawn.
There is still so much to say,
Yet words seem so cold and cliché,
'Don't go! We will miss you! Forever is a long time!'
And yet as you labour hard to breathe,
Hurry on now so you can find peace,
And rest at last, my beloved father.

Georgia Thompson (13)
Wrekin College, Wellington

Young Writers
Est. 1991

YOUNG WRITERS INFORMATION

We hope you have enjoyed reading this book – and that you will continue to in the coming years.

If you're a young writer who enjoys reading and creative writing, or the parent of an enthusiastic poet or story writer, do visit our website www.youngwriters.co.uk. Here you will find free competitions, workshops and games, as well as recommended reads, a poetry glossary and our blog.

If you would like to order further copies of this book, or any of our other titles give us a call or visit **www.youngwriters.co.uk**.

Young Writers
Remus House
Coltsfoot Drive
Peterborough
PE2 9BF

(01733) 890066
info@youngwriters.co.uk